TRACING YOUR MERCHANT NAVY ANCESTORS

FAMILY HISTORY FROM PEN & SWORD

TRACING YOUR MERCHANT NAVY ANCESTORS

A Guide for Family Historians

Simon Wills

Pen & Sword
FAMILY HISTORY

First published in Great Britain in 2012 by
PEN & SWORD FAMILY HISTORY
an imprint of
Pen & Sword Books Ltd
47 Church Street
Barnsley
South Yorkshire
S70 2AS

ISBN 978 1 84884 651 7

A CIP catalogue record for this book is
available from the British Library.

Typeset in Palatino and Optima by
Phoenix Typesetting, Auldgirth, Dumfriesshire

Printed and bound in England by
CPI Group (UK) Ltd, Croydon, CR0 4YY

Pen & Sword Books Ltd incorporates the imprints of
Pen & Sword Aviation, Pen & Sword Family History, Pen & Sword Maritime,
Pen & Sword Military, Pen & Sword Discovery, Wharncliffe Local History,
Wharncliffe True Crime, Wharncliffe Transport, Pen & Sword Select,
Pen & Sword Military Classics, Leo Cooper, The Praetorian Press,
Remember When, Seaforth Publishing and Frontline Publishing

For a complete list of Pen & Sword titles please contact
PEN & SWORD BOOKS LIMITED
47 Church Street, Barnsley, South Yorkshire, S70 2AS, England
E-mail: enquiries@pen-and-sword.co.uk
Website: www.pen-and-sword.co.uk

CONTENTS

To Dad,
who taught me to love the sea

PREFACE

The merchant navy has been vital to Britain's prosperity, identity, and worldwide influence. Although the phrase 'merchant navy' suggests that it is one large organisation, it has always consisted of many separate entities, ranging from an individual owning a single ship to large shipping companies with enormous fleets at their disposal. Whatever their size, merchant navy organisations are all focused on the means by which ships can yield a commercial profit from the sea.

Merchant ships initially employed only seamen, with officers such as captains to control them, but the growth of the industry, coupled with technological advancement, meant that new roles emerged in the nineteenth century. When sail gave way to ships with engines, engineers were needed. When large passenger ships began to ply the seas, staff were needed to cater for the public's needs while on board. So a career in the merchant service has not necessarily meant becoming a seaman or ship's officer.

It is very common when researching a British family tree to find ancestors who went to sea because such huge numbers of people were employed in the merchant service. Once you find one seafarer, though, you may find many because it was a career that often ran in families: fathers took their sons to sea with them to teach them what they knew. A seagoing career was mainly confined to men until the twentieth century.

Compared to many other occupations, the delight for family historians researching merchant navy employees is that so much information has survived, especially after 1835. However, this apparent benefit may be a problem for the newcomer because, with so much information available, it can be difficult to know where to start. In this book, I have tried to be practical and focus the reader's attention on the subjects that people most commonly want to investigate. For example, you may already know that your fore-bear was a captain, or have recently found that a relative was a seaman, so there are chapters devoted to these two topics to guide you through the sources available to take your research further. I have found that most family historians want to know more about the individual ships that their ancestors served on but it can be difficult to find advice about how to do this, consequently I was particularly keen to include a chapter about it. I have also always been intrigued by family tales that have survived down the generations, and yarns about shipwrecks and gallantry at sea are some of the most exciting, so there is a chapter that looks at this area. Finally, I have offered advice on how to explore the war service of merchant navy employees.

Where at all possible, I have guided you towards sources of information on the internet in the first instance. Good-quality web resources will often save you a great deal of time because they are usually indexed by name, and do not require you to travel in order to access information. However, you will probably need to visit The National Archives (TNA) in London at some point. Their holdings of merchant navy records are unrivalled, but do prepare carefully before you go by reading their online Research Guides. These can all be found on the TNA website, www.national archives.gov.uk, and are indexed under 'Merchant Seamen' and 'Merchant Shipping'. However, this book introduces you to the many resources held by other organisations that can also help you take your researches further.

You will note that throughout the book I have tended to prefer the word 'captain' to describe the man in charge of a ship because it is the word that most people know, but historically this figure was often referred to as the ship's master.

The challenge of researching a merchant navy ancestor is essentially to understand what resources are available and then to adopt a methodical approach to hunting through them. In this respect, I hope this book will be your trusty guide and companion, and that you will enjoy using it as much as I have enjoyed writing it.

Chapter 1

BRITAIN'S MERCHANT FLEET

The merchant navy consists of ships that ply the seas for commercial reasons. This includes passenger ships, cargo ships, support vessels (e.g. tugs), and fishing vessels. This book is not concerned with fishermen, who are considered in a companion publication: Martin Wilcox's *Fishing and Fishermen: A Guide for Family Historians* (Pen & Sword, 2009).

The service was given the prestigious name of 'Merchant Navy' by King George V in 1922 as a sign of the nation's gratitude for the great courage shown by its crews in the First World War. Before this time, it was variously known as the merchant or mercantile service, marine, or fleet. The merchant navy's flag is the red ensign (or 'red duster'), which has an even older heritage: it was a former Royal Navy flag that was made exclusive to British-registered merchant ships in 1864. It is pictured on the front cover of this book.

Maritime Domination

Merchant shipping has proved vital to the economy of Britain. In the nineteenth century, as Britain consolidated a worldwide empire, the merchant service expanded dramatically and was the principal mechanism behind Britain's position at the centre of world trade. By 1826 the merchant service already employed 160,000 seagoing crewmen, compared to only 21,000 employed by the Royal Navy, whose crews had slumped to a sixth of their Napoleonic-era levels.

When researching seafaring ancestors, it helps to know the main centres of maritime activity. In 1835, the ten UK ports with most registered merchant ships over 15 tons were:

1. London (2,663 ships)
2. Newcastle (987)

1

3. Liverpool (805)
4. Sunderland (624)
5. Yarmouth, Isle of Wight (585)
6. Hull (579)
7. Whitehaven, Cumbria (496)
8. Beaumaris, Anglesey (389)
9. Greenock, Inverclyde (371)
10. Aberdeen (350)

It is interesting to note that Southampton, which many readers might expect to see listed here, did not rise to eminence until the late nineteenth century.

By the 1840s around 40 per cent of all merchant ships worldwide were registered in the British Empire, with four new ships being built to join the fleet *every day* in some years.

At the end of the nineteenth century, the overwhelming dominance of the British in world merchant shipping can be seen by examining the numbers of vessels registered in each nation. In 1899 there were 10,998 British-registered steam or sailing ships over 100 tons. Even discounting the two thousand or so of these that operated from ports outside the UK, Britain's merchant fleet dwarfed its closest mercantile rival the USA, which had only 2,739 seagoing ships. The next five largest nations were Norway (2,528 ships), Germany (1,676), Sweden (1,408), Russia (1,218), and France (1,183). Even in 1950, there were still 9,124 British-registered ships, although Britain's position in the league table of ship-owning nations had slipped to second when classified by carrying capacity (tonnage), behind the USA.

Managing the Service

In terms of personnel, the merchant navy consists of the collective crews that operate merchant ships, under a variety of owners. It is not a single organisation like the Royal Navy. However, the sheer scale of the operation has provoked various attempts to coordinate or control the merchant service nationally. It is important for family historians to have some understanding of this because it dictates where to look for information about an ancestor.

There has always been a relationship between Britain's military and civilian fleets, not least because in wartime the Royal Navy needed crewmen and the merchant navy sought protection.

Consequently, at various points in time, Admiralty records are valuable to the family historian researching merchant navy ancestors. For example, it was the Admiralty that ran press gangs or provided warships to escort merchant convoys. Some of your ancestors, of course, may have been employed by both services.

The various attempts to register seamen and ships, which began in the eighteenth century, were overseen by a registrar. The post of Registrar General of Shipping, created in 1786, was attached to the Board of Customs. When the registration of seamen commenced, this became the responsibility of the Board of Trade which was originally a consultative committee, but became an executive and regulator. From 1850, the Registrar General of Shipping and Seamen (RGSS) became the regulator for vessels and crews alike.

In 1916, the Ministry of Shipping was created to control merchant shipping during the First World War. The ministry was dissolved in 1921, and its responsibilities were again taken up by the Board of Trade. In 1939, the Ministry of Shipping was recreated, but was subsumed into the Ministry of War Transport in 1941. In 1946 this became simply the Ministry of Transport, which thereafter retained a governmental remit for merchant shipping, although it is now called the Department for Transport, www.dft.gov.uk.

Shipping Companies

Although some large shipping companies existed before 1800, most merchant vessels were privately owned by individuals or small consortia of local businessmen until the middle of the nineteenth century. Technology was an important factor in changing this, particularly the adoption of the steam engine, and this is discussed in more detail below. Nonetheless, once shipowners acquired sizeable fleets, they looked to establish an identity for their business. They did this by creating a brand, which was promoted by ships' names and appearances, crew uniforms, and advertising. Companies tried to ensure their ships could be clearly identified by their house flags (e.g. Lambert Brothers sported a white flag with a central red triangle), distinctive funnels (e.g. Clan Line ships were black with two red bands), and hulls (e.g. Orient Line ships were corn coloured). The FlagSpot website provides illustrations of house flags wich may help you identify owners from photographs of ships; choose 'flags of shipping

Corporate identity: The 'T' on this cargo ship's funnel indicates her ownership by the Tatem Steam Navigation Company of Cardiff.

companies' from the subject index http://flagspot.net. Many companies also ensured that their ships' names had a corporate feel – for instance, vessels belonging to the White Star Line all ended in -ic (e.g. *Titanic, Olympic*), whereas Cunard ships tended to end in -ia or to be named after British queens (e.g. *Carpathia, Queen Elizabeth*). Famous British shipping companies included Blue Funnel, Cunard, Ellerman, the Peninsular & Oriental Steam Navigation Co (P&O), Union-Castle, and the White Star Line.

Unfortunately, most collections of shipping company records are incomplete. The National Maritime Museum (NMM) at Greenwich has the company records for around thirty commercial shipping organisations including Devitt & Moore and P&O, and they are listed in an online Research Guide at www.nmm.ac.uk/researchers/library/research-guides/. Although many consist principally of accounts and other business records, some do identify sailing schedules and members of staff. P&O has loaned its records to the NMM, but its own website provides a very detailed guide to the records available, www.poheritage.com.

Another archive which maintains an impressive collection of shipping company records is the Merseyside Maritime Museum Archive in Liverpool. This houses selected records for companies such as the Ellerman Line, Pacific Steam Navigation Company, Elder Dempster, and Cunard.

Records for the East India Company are kept in the Asia, Pacific and Africa Collections at the British Library (reference IOR). The original captain's journals are indexed alphabetically by ship's name and date back to the early seventeenth century, but there are also appointment and service records for officers. However, a number of other sources can help you begin your research into this company, its ships, and its employees without travelling to the British Library. For example, the website www.eicships.info lists all East India Company ships and their captains, and is constructing a database of seagoing East India employees. *Lloyd's Register* includes an annual list of the company's ships from 1778 to 1833. Google Books http://books.google.com provides the full text of *A Register of Ships Employed in the Service of the Honorable the United East India Company from the Year 1760 to 1810* by Charles Hardy. This valuable book lists all the company's ships and their officers, together with voyages made.

Records for shipping companies in other regional archives can sometimes be found by using the online index Access To Archives at www.nationalarchives.gov.uk/a2a/. If this is unsuccessful and you know where a shipping line was based in the UK, it is worth contacting the nearest regional archive to see if it holds records or knows of their location. Bear in mind that over the years there have been many takeovers and amalgamations, so you may need to look for historical records under the name of the most recent owner. Companies that still exist usually know where their historical records are held. Finally, books about individual companies may assist you – all the principal maritime archives have good collections, although Merseyside and the NMM have the largest.

Sailing Ships

The earliest ships used for trade were paddled in rivers or coastal shallows using oars. The advent of the sail allowed vessels to travel farther from home and faster. For the non-expert, the terminology used to describe sailing vessels can be confusing, which is unfortunate because most family historians simply want to know what an ancestor's ship looked like. Sometimes a picture of a named ship can be found (see Chapter 3), but most of the time this is not possible.

There were five principal sailing ships used for trade that family historians will encounter, and the descriptions below are accompanied by illustrations on the following pages.

Barque

The largest of the sailing ships, barques usually carried three or four masts. The stern-most mast was 'fore and aft rigged', comprising triangular sails that ran broadly in line with the hull. The other masts were all 'square rigged', which meant that the square-ish sails were carried on 'yards' crossing each mast at right angles. The similar 'barquentine' was square-rigged on the first mast only. Barques tended to be used for oceangoing transport. In the later nineteenth century, some very large barques carried up to five masts and were known as 'windjammers'.

A four-masted barque.

The popular brig was employed widely.

A schooner.

The slim and streamlined clipper.

Brig

This popular workhorse of the eighteenth and early nineteenth centuries was fast and manoeuvrable. It carried two square-rigged masts, but the second mast (mainmast) sported a fore-and-aft-rigged sail as well. Although definitions have changed over time, the similar 'brigantine' was a two-masted ship with only one mast square-rigged (the foremast). Another variation on the brig was called a 'snow'. Brigs were used for coastal trade as well as ocean-going transport.

Clipper

These fast oceangoing ships had slim hulls to ease passage through the water and three square-rigged masts.

Cutter and Sloop

Nowadays, these vessels both tend to be single-masted and yacht-size, rigged fore-and-aft, and differing in how far forward the mast is carried. Yet over the centuries the terms 'sloop' and 'cutter' have referred to various types of craft. Interestingly, there has often been

A cutter.

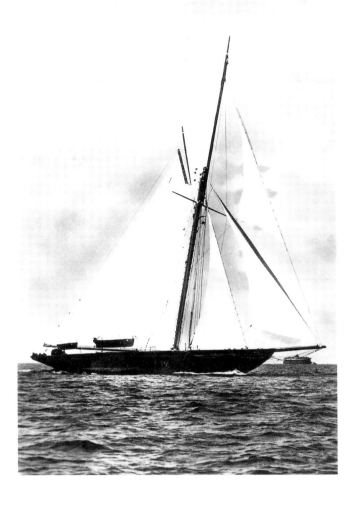

a marked difference between how the terms were used in the merchant navy and Royal Navy, and definitions have also varied with the era. Even within the merchant service the number of masts and sails could vary, and the word 'cutter' could mean something different to, for example, a ship's pilot or a fisherman. Probably the most that can be said here, without giving a long history of the two terms, is that these merchant vessels were small, fore-and-aft rigged, and often sported a single mast. To understand precisely what a specific cutter or sloop looked like, you really need to view the ship's registration document (see Chapter 3) or a picture. Cutters and sloops were used principally for coastal travel and short trips to Continental Europe.

Schooner

Schooners usually carried two or three masts, but some carried as many as seven. The most notable feature was that all masts were fore-and-aft rigged. Like brigs, schooners were used for coastal or ocean voyages.

Ships with Engines

Sailing ships had two significant disadvantages. Firstly, they were dependent on the wind for propulsion – a free power source but an unpredictable one – so sailing ships could be slow or unreliable. Secondly, big sailing ships demanded a comparatively large crew, so they were expensive to operate, especially when the costs of constant repairs and upkeep of things such as rigging were factored in. The traditional wooden hull and decks of sailing ships leaked as well, which threatened the integrity of some cargoes.

In the nineteenth century a number of changes in technology and ship design came about within a relatively short period of time. Most radically, the advent of the steam engine meant that for the first time ships could operate without reliance on the wind. The first steamships were built in the eighteenth century, but it was not until the nineteenth that they crossed oceans and gained widespread acceptance. They initially burned coal as their source of power.

The first ship with a steam engine to cross the Atlantic was the American vessel SS *Savannah* in 1819, although its engines were only used for a small part of the voyage, the majority still being under sail. An attachment to the old ways meant that oceangoing steamships carried both engine and sails for many decades to come; it took time to generate confidence that steam power alone was sufficiently trustworthy. Brunel's SS *Great Western* was the first steamship built for the purpose of crossing the Atlantic regularly and it began its scheduled runs in 1838. Yet this ship still had a wooden hull, and the method of propulsion was via a paddle wheel on the side of the ship.

The iron hull gave ships greater strength and durability, and was

A steamer with a paddle wheel rather than a propeller.

cheaper than wood. The screw propeller allowed ships to reach greater speeds than a paddle wheel and was easier to build and maintain. These two innovations came to the fore simultaneously in the 1840s, even though the benefits of both had been known for some time. The first man to put together steam engine plus iron hull plus screw propeller successfully for the purpose of crossing the ocean was, predictably, Brunel with his SS *Great Britain*. From this point onwards, steamships grew rapidly in numbers and size. By 1860, there were over half a million British-registered steamers.

The advent of fast and strong steamships did not mark the immediate demise of sail; for example, it remained more economical to use small, lightly crewed sailing ships for coastal trade for many decades. At the same time, sailing ships themselves continued to evolve. For example, in the 1840s clipper ships had a new sleek hull design that speeded the passage of sailing ships across oceans. Some sailing ships began to grow in size, and many were built with iron frames, iron hulls, or iron plating over wood.

When the Suez Canal opened in 1869, it offered a significant shortcut for engine-driven ships that travelled between Europe and Asia, but the canal was not so easy for sailing ships to use. In the second half of the century, steel started to replace iron as the main metal for shipbuilding since it is stronger. Another important advance was the use of more than one propeller, which gave steamships even greater speed.

Ships with engines had become firmly established as the norm by the end of the nineteenth century, and with the arrival of the steam turbine they became faster and more reliable. Yet large ocean-crossing sailing ships continued to operate on a limited basis until the early years of the twentieth century. They were used mainly to transport heavy, bulk international cargoes that were not perishable, such as wool, timber, and wine. As a consequence, sailing ships grew in size so that greater quantities of cargo could be transported: the so-called 'windjammers' carried up to five masts and forty-seven sails. The German ship *Preussen* was the

ORIENT LINE
FORTNIGHTLY MAIL SERVICE
BETWEEN
ENGLAND AND AUSTRALIA.

AUSTRAL	LUSITANIA	ORIENT	ORMUZ	OROYA
5524 tons. 7000 h.p.	3877 tons. 4000 h.p.	5365 tons. 6000 h.p.	6031 tons. 8500 h.p.	6297 tons. 7000 h.p.
CUZCO	OPHIR	ORIZABA	OROTAVA	ORUBA
3918 tons. 4000 h.p.	6910 tons. 10,000 h.p.	6077 tons. 7000 h.p.	5552 tons. 7000 h.p.	5552 tons. 7000 h.p.

CALLING TO LAND AND EMBARK PASSENGERS AT

GIBRALTAR, NAPLES, PORT SAID, SUEZ, COLOMBO, ALBANY, ADELAIDE, MELBOURNE, AND SYDNEY.

Passengers booked on through tickets for all ports in Australia, Tasmania, and New Zealand.

High-class Cuisine. Electric Lighting. Hot and Cold Baths, good Ventilation, and every Comfort.

CHEAP SINGLE AND RETURN TICKETS.

*Managers :—*F. GREEN & CO., 13, Fenchurch Avenue,
ANDERSON, ANDERSON & CO., 5, Fenchurch Avenue, } LONDON, E.C.

For FREIGHT or PASSAGE apply to the latter Firm at 5, FENCHURCH AVENUE, E.C.,
Or at the West End Branch Office:—16, COCKSPUR STREET, S.W.

Engine power made possible scheduled voyages as this late 1880s advertisement shows. Even at this date, the steamship pictured still carried masts.

12

largest, with a gross tonnage of over 5,000 tons. Across very long distances – such as the Europe to Australia route – they remained, for a time, an economical option.

The speed with which engines took over from sail can be seen by comparing the types of registered ships in the British Empire over a crucial fifty-year period. In 1860, there were over four million registered sailing ships and around 500,000 steamships over 100 tons. By 1910, there were still over a million sailing vessels, but more than eleven million steamships.

In the twentieth century, oil began to take over from coal as a source of fuel for steam engines, and in the latter half of the century diesel engines made their appearance.

An important consequence of the rise of engine-powered vessels was that ships' arrivals and departures became more predictable than they had been in the days of sail. As a result, many owners could advertise a regular sailing schedule with times and routes specified in advance. These ships became known as 'liners'. Vessels that did not follow pre-set sailing times and routes were known as tramp ships.

Cargo Ships

Merchant ships have gradually increased their speeds and their capacity for carrying cargoes so that large quantities of goods can now be carried across the oceans. When ships were made of wood, an important consideration for merchants was the integrity of a ship's hull, because leaks allowed seawater into the hold, where it could potentially ruin cargos. Publications such as Lloyd's Register (see Chapter 3) helped merchants decide on the suitability of a particular ship for the goods they wished transported. A fast, new ship with a strong hull might be used to carry perishable fruit or luxury items, whereas older, slower ships more prone to leaks might carry bulk, hardy goods such as coal or stone.

Not all cargoes were legitimate – merchant navy personnel indulged in their fair share of smuggling, and some ships were fitted with special hideaway places to store illicit goods, particularly in the eighteenth century. It should also be noted that some cargo ships continued to carry small numbers of passengers right into the twentieth century, albeit in more primitive conditions than on purpose-built passenger ships.

Until the twentieth century, most cargo ships did not sail

according to a fixed schedule. For example, a ship would be paid to deliver goods from port A to port B, perhaps by several different merchants. On arrival, the cargo would be unloaded and the captain would already have a return cargo to load, or would seek one, to avoid wasting a voyage home empty. The new cargo might require a direct return trip to port A, but it could involve a detour to somewhere else *en route*. The scope available for such diversions depended on the conditions under which the crew were hired, the owner's instructions to the captain, and any other commitments awaiting the ship in its port of origin.

Across the last three centuries, some cargoes are ubiquitous: grain, spices, wine, tea, coal, timber, and china. Others are associated with particular eras. In the eighteenth century, for example, you will commonly find records of the carriage of animal furs from North America and products of the British whaling industry. The bulk carriage of international mail by sea only began in the nineteenth century, whereas large oil tankers rose to prominence in the twentieth century. Cargo ships have adapted over time to fulfil the role required of them – essentially they have transported progressively more goods as quickly as possible (e.g. container ships) or specialised goods (e.g. refrigerated ships).

Passenger Ships

Although this section deals primarily with ships that carried fare-paying passengers, it should not be forgotten that in its history the merchant service has carried people in other circumstances, including convicts, troops, evacuees, and slaves.

Early long-distance passenger ships such as the *Mayflower* were cargo ships crudely refitted to transport people. Passengers would have been accommodated below decks in hastily demarcated small spaces with very little privacy. These were dark, damp, smelly, and airless – stifling in the summer and freezing in the winter. Journeys would have been uncomfortable, slow, and monotonous – yet terrifying during a storm, when everyone and everything would have been thrown about in the dark, below decks. Passengers were left to take care of themselves unless they brought servants with them. The primitive food consisted mainly of dry rations that would not deteriorate on long voyages, such as ship's biscuits, salt meat and fish, dried peas, cereals, beer, sugar, and perhaps cheese and raisins. Cooking made this meagre diet only a little more appetising.

Even in the nineteenth century, some passengers had to provide their own food for a voyage, and those who did not (or ran out) were often charged extortionate prices whilst at sea. It was not until the 1849 Passenger Act that shipowners were obliged to provide transatlantic passengers with sufficient food and water. Transatlantic ships with more than one hundred passengers had also to provide a cook and a doctor.

In the days of sail the time to reach a destination was unpredictable. It took the *Mayflower* sixty-six days to cross the Atlantic in 1620, but even two hundred years later passengers on sailing ships endured similar times. Masters of Victorian sailing ships were instructed to assume the transatlantic passage would take ten weeks for the purposes of provisioning the ship. So when, in 1845, Brunel's steamship *Great Britain* did the journey in fourteen days at a speed of around 11 knots it must have seemed like a miracle.

Shipowners readily appreciated the advantages of speed – faster ships could fit in more voyages per year – but capacity was the next hurdle. The *Great Britain* carried 360 passengers. This was a significant improvement on sailing vessels, but not a very economical number given the expense of building, fuelling, and crewing the steamship. The *Great Britain*'s crew numbered around 130, whereas sailing ship crews were usually less than half this. Bigger ships would carry more passengers and would be more cost-effective, so passenger ships began to increase in size.

Perhaps because they initially focused on speed and capacity, it took some time for shipowners to appreciate that the public would pay for comfortable shipboard accommodation, rather than put up with the bare essentials. The White Star Line's *Oceanic* established something of a precedent in this respect. It was launched in 1870, was 3,707 tons, and carried 1,166 passengers and 143 crew. *Oceanic* was sumptuously decorated, had the novelty of running water, and sported extra-large portholes. The ship broke with tradition by carrying all its first-class passengers amidships, where there was less engine vibration, instead of in the stern, which was formerly considered the prestigious place for persons of wealth to be accommodated. Cunard's ship *Servia*, 7,392 tons, was launched in 1881 and was the first ship lit by electric lights.

Vessels continued to increase in size, luxury, and speed. By the end of the nineteenth century, after engine redesigns and the use of screw propellers, you could cross the Atlantic in less than six days.

The 21,000-ton *Celtic* was launched by the White Star Line in 1901 to carry an unprecedented 2,857 passengers. This was the largest ship afloat at the time and its size gave space for novel passenger luxuries such as swimming baths, gymnasia, saunas and veranda cafés. Competition between the shipping companies intensified, resulting in a whole range of famous liners – ever-increasing in size, luxury, and the range of services they offered passengers. All this resulted in significantly larger crews. The *Mauretania* was launched in 1906 and was the fastest and largest ship afloat at the time, achieving record speeds of 24 knots and with a gross tonnage of 32,000. The 52,000-ton *Imperator* carried a previously unheard of 4,000 passengers and 1,100 crew. The first five decades of the twentieth century were the golden age of the liner: the famed *Olympic*, *Bremen*, *Aquitania*, *Normandie*, *Oronsay*, and *Queen Elizabeth*, and the ill-fated *Titanic*, *Lusitania* and *Laconia* were all launched in this period.

For many people, the *Queen Mary* represents the pinnacle of the British liner era. Launched in 1934, its gross tonnage was 81,235, and it attained record transatlantic speeds of around 31 knots that stood for fourteen years. Amazingly, the *Queen Mary* continued to ply the oceans until 1967, but the advent of long-distance air

A luxury suite on a 1920s liner.

travel from the late 1950s sounded the death knell for most ocean liners.

The largest British-registered passenger liner currently operating is the *Queen Mary 2*, with a gross tonnage of 148,528. It has seventeen decks, carries 3,056 passengers, a crew of 1,253, and has a top speed of around 28.5 knots.

Chapter 2

LIFE IN THE MERCHANT SERVICE

The facilities on a merchant ship vary greatly according to the era and the vessel's purpose. In the days of sail, they were rudimentary. There was no electricity, no heating, no running water. This meant that toilets, or 'heads', for example, were simply holes cut into the bows of the ship hanging over the sea, although passengers might use a potty.

The diet was basic and consisted of dried foods ('vittles') that could be stored for long periods without deteriorating, although some ships took livestock with them and had fresh fruit and vegetables at the start of a voyage. Sometimes fish would be caught during the voyage to supplement the diet as well. There was one small kitchen ('galley') with a range for cooking.

The quarters for seamen consisted of hammocks slung below decks, generally in the forecastle at the front of the ship, which took the worst of the seas and weather. Hammocks were folded away when not in use or brought up onto the maindeck for airing. A seaman's possessions were kept in a lockable sea chest that was also stored in the forecastle. The senior officers would have cabins at the rear of the vessel – the captain's being large enough for a desk, a bunk-style bed, windows, and space to receive and dine other officers or passengers. As ship design progressed, some sailing ships had rooms ('deck houses') with bunks on the maindeck for senior members of the crew.

Religion was particularly important in the Victorian era. It is a generalisation, but seamen tended to be superstitious, and were keen not to do anything that might tempt fate. Given the vicissitudes of the weather at sea, this is understandable. Paying one's due respects to God was part of this ethos, and so time was set aside for religious observance, led by the captain, every Sunday.

A kitchen or 'galley' on an 1870s sailing ship.

The extent and frequency of religious observance was largely determined by his piety or otherwise.

It was important for efficiency and safety to keep the ship clean, organised, and tidy ('ship shape') – this meant that a significant proportion of a seaman's duties at sea involved repair and maintenance. They also needed to find time to mend and wash their own clothes. Any spare time might be spent in conversation, gambling, smoking, dancing, singing, playing instruments, carving, and writing letters or reading.

Some sailing ships carried arms to deter pirates or the enemy in times of war. However, unless the vessel was a privateer (see

Chapter 7), ordnance usually consisted of a few cannon and small arms, although every seaman carried his own knife. Merchant seamen were generally not skilled in the use of firearms. (This changed in the world wars, when some merchant ships were armed and crews trained to use them.)

Beyond the era of sail, living conditions started to improve dramatically. Large steel ships meant proper sleeping bunks for crews and more privacy; electricity allowed lighting and refrigeration so that fresh provisions could be kept longer; running water improved personal hygiene.

However, a long-running problem well into the twentieth century was that seamen and officers alike were employed for one voyage at a time, and could be discharged when it ended. Having said this, many men did gain long-term employment with the same shipowner but were not paid unless they were working on board. When a ship needed repairs or a refit, for example, owners did not pay a captain and crew to stand idle while the shipyard went to work: they all had to find employment elsewhere. This lack of job security led to fluctuations in income and career fortunes.

From 1845, crews at least received written agreements summarising their terms of employment (see Chapter 4). Before formal agreements were introduced, shipowners and captains alike were capable of gross abuses – perhaps most notably in terms of the punishments they could get away with. Once agreements existed, crewmen were expected to 'conduct themselves in an orderly, faithful, sober and honest manner and to be at all times diligent in their respective duties'. In return, owners had to describe pay, hours of work, punishments, and the food provided. Discipline was largely enforced by fines deducted from pay owing, but men could also be barred from future employment, confined below decks, or 'disrated' (lowered in rank) and given menial duties. Ultimately, crewmembers could be arrested and subjected to legal proceedings once ashore if necessary. Examples of behaviour that would have been punished in the nineteenth century included:

- Striking or assaulting anyone on board
- Drunkenness
- Possessing a firearm or offensive weapon without permission
- Insolent or contemptuous language or behaviour; swearing
- Disobedience to lawful commands
- Absence without leave

- Theft or damage of cargo
- Negligence (e.g. sleeping while on watch)
- Not attending divine worship on Sundays or behaving inappropriately on Sundays

Desertion, running, or 'jumping ship' was quite common. Seamen forfeited their wages on their previous ship if they did this, as well as any possessions they left behind. Seamen who deserted usually sought voyage destinations, disciplinary regimes, or crewmates that were more to their liking rather than to leave the service completely, although some wanted to explore a new country or settle in it.

For most crewmembers, longer-term contracts beyond a single voyage did not emerge until the mid-twentieth century.

Navigation and Time

Navigation and time-keeping are vital responsibilities on board and deserve special mention. Early ships rarely sailed away from land because they had a limited ability to navigate other than by following coastal landmarks. At night, stars could be used to show the broad direction of travel, as could the path of the sun during the day.

The first compasses were used in Europe in the Middle Ages, and consisted of a suspended piece of naturally occurring lodestone, an iron-containing mineral that tends to orientate to magnetic north. Latitude could be calculated by measuring the distance of the pole star above the horizon at night or of the sun above the horizon at noon. Instruments used to measure this included the cross-staff, quadrant, octant, and sextant.

It was not until the eighteenth century that a ship's position by longitude (or meridian lines) could be measured, as this required the use of very reliable clocks called chronometers. A knowledge of both latitude and longitude was needed both to create accurate maps and to use them.

Merchant navy records often refer to units of distance which are not always familiar to landsmen. They include:

- Cable – this has varied in its definition, but is usually a tenth of a nautical mile
- Fathom – 6 feet

- League – 3 nautical miles
- Nautical mile – currently equal to 1.15 miles or 1.85 kilometres

The speed of a ship is expressed in nautical miles per hour or 'knots'. In the days of sail this was determined by the following method. A quadrant-shaped wooden board was thrown off the stern of the ship, attached to a line on a reel. This was known as a log. At the same time an egg-timer was turned. The line had knots tied into it at set intervals, and these were counted as they passed over the side. The distance between the knots was proportionate to 1 nautical mile, and so the number that ran out before the egg-timer stopped enabled speed to be calculated.

Time on board ship was sounded via a series of bells. From noon, there were seven 'watch' periods in the ensuing 24 hours when an officer or senior crewman took charge of the main deck and was responsible for navigating the ship and posting lookouts. The watches were:

Afternoon watch	Noon to 4:00 p.m.
First dogwatch	4:00 p.m. to 6:00 p.m.

The line and log used to measure a sailing ship's speed. One of the knots on the reel can be seen tagged with a white strip of cloth to mark a set distance.

Second dogwatch	6:00 p.m. to 8:00 p.m.
First watch	8:00 p.m. to midnight
Middle or mid watch	Midnight to 4:00 a.m.
Morning watch	4:00 a.m. to 8:00 a.m.
Forenoon watch	8:00 a.m. to noon

A loud bell was rung once after the first 30 minutes of each watch, then twice after one hour, three times after an hour and a half, and so on until 'eight bells', which indicated the end of a four-hour watch. These audible cues meant there was no excuse for anyone not being on duty when they were supposed to be.

A Career at Sea

Roles in the Merchant Service

There have been many different responsibilities on board merchant ships in varying eras, and it is not possible to identify all those roles here. There are, for example, many jobs that are almost identical to their shore-based counterparts (e.g. waiter). However, the more commonly encountered roles that you will see identified in contemporary records are outlined below.

Apprentice ('A' or 'App')
Young teenagers from the age of about twelve could be granted an apprenticeship to pursue an agreed duration of training to become a seaman or officer. After 1823, it became obligatory for ships weighing more than 80 tons to carry at least one apprentice. See Chapter 4 for details of apprenticeship records.

Boatswain ('Bos')
Also spelled 'bosun', this was the most senior seaman on board. The role included supervising the seamen on deck, allocating tasks to them, ensuring work was completed properly, and motivating or disciplining the crew.

Boy
Although some youths took apprenticeships in the days of sail, other young men around the age of twelve to sixteen could go to sea as boys, without the promise of formal training, to perform

menial tasks around the ship, hoping to gain enough experience to become a seaman in due course.

Captain ('C')

The captain was usually called the ship's master ('M^r' or 'Mstr') in the merchant service, but sometimes the commander, and on small ships often referred to as 'skipper'. The captain has overall responsibility for the conduct of the crew, safety, and navigation. The most senior captain in a large shipping company may be termed 'commodore'.

Carpenter ('Cptr')

In the age of sail, this was a specialist who effected essential repairs and maintenance to keep the ship afloat. The role persisted even when ships were made of steel because wood was still widely used in construction for things such as deck housing and lifeboats.

Cook ('Ck')

By the beginning of the twentieth century the position of cook was recognised as one with important safety implications. To ensure professional competence, a national certification scheme was introduced (see Chapter 4). In large ships there was more than one cook and a series of support staff. There could also be food preparation specialists such as bakers or butchers.

Donkeyman

This was the most senior rating in the engine room, often an older crewman.

Engineer ('E' or 'Engr')

These officers are responsible for the ship's engines and other machinery on board ship (e.g. winches, fridges). The most senior is the chief engineer, and he reports to the captain directly. He may have a deputy called the assistant chief engineer; others are numbered for seniority – second engineer ('2E'), third engineer ('3E'), etc. There is never a first engineer.

Fireman ('F')

He stoked the fires on a ship fuelled by coal. Those who filled both fireman and trimmer roles (see below) are often documented as

'F&T'. Some firemen progressed to become greasers. The term 'stoker' was used for a similar role in the Royal Navy.

Greaser ('Gsr')
These were attendants under the control of an engineer, and lubricated, cleaned, and helped repair machinery.

Gunner ('Gnr')
He was responsible for the ship's principal armament as carried by, for example, a privateer in the age of sail or an armed merchant ship in the world wars (in this latter case often a Royal Navy employee).

Lamp Trimmer
He kept the oil lamps burning efficiently.

Mate and Deck Officers
Smaller ships generally had one mate who reported to the captain, but larger vessels had a first mate ('1M') who was the captain's deputy, then a second mate ('2M') and so on, numbered for seniority. In more modern times, the most senior mate has been called the chief officer (or chief mate, 'C/M'), who has a first, second, third officer, etc. reporting to him. Apprentice or trainee officers were often called cadets or sometimes midshipmen, and newly qualified officers were junior officers.

Medical Officer
The 'MO' was sometimes called 'doctor' or 'surgeon' (mainly in the age of sail), and in more modern times has been assisted by nurses or matrons.

Purser ('Purs')
This officer is responsible for a myriad of tasks connected with the ship's supplies, crew's wages, clerical work, and passenger comfort. This includes the red tape of immigration, the mail, shore excursions for passengers, complaints, payment for food and stores, etc. On a large ship there may be more than one, so a chief purser ('CP') is appointed.

Quartermaster ('QM')

This position was found on large ships and was often filled by an older, more experienced seaman. The role included steering the ship in compliance with an officer's orders and otherwise assisting with navigation.

Seaman ('S')

Also known as mariners, they crew the ship, undertake maintenance roles, and secure the ship's cargo. Ordinary seamen ('OS' or 'Ord') are relatively newly appointed and lack some key skills, whereas able seamen are more experienced and would be expected to undertake additional duties such as standing watch and taking the helm. Able seamen are usually identified by the abbreviations 'AB', 'AM' or 'Able'.

Steward or Stewardesses ('Stwd')

The most senior is the chief steward/stewardess who is an officer, and is assisted by a team of stewards and stewardesses to meet the needs of passengers.

Storekeeper ('Strkpr')

He was responsible for the safe housing of the ship's stores of food, water, clothing, and other essentials.

Telegrapher, Wireless Operator and Radio Officer

These communications officers or 'sparks' worked initially using Morse code, but then moved to voice transmission when radio was introduced. They were employed as early as 1900, and the role is often abbreviated in records to 'W/O' or 'R/O'. In the first half of the twentieth century some shipping companies employed their own personnel, but many were recruited from wireless companies, which supplied both the trained operator and the equipment (e.g. those employed by the Marconi International Marine Communications Company Ltd were known as 'Marconi men').

Trimmer ('T' or 'Trmr')

He ensured that the fireman had sufficient coal for stoking the ship's fires, and cleared away ash. The trimmer also managed the ship's coal stocks so that they were run down evenly in storage areas, otherwise the imbalance caused by an uneven load could allow the ship to 'lose its trim'.

Roles for Women at Sea

Some Victorian shipping companies employed women in shore-based roles such as secretarial positions, but there was little opportunity for women to go to sea. Interestingly, there are a number of newspaper reports of women dressing as men to try and secure such a role throughout the nineteenth century. For example, the *Leeds Mercury* for 19 January 1860 reports this story:

A FEMALE SAILOR. – At the Rochdale police court, yesterday, Tom Stewart being called, a stout person about nineteen years of age, dressed like a genuine sailor, stepped into the dock. Superintendent Callendar stated that a constable was on duty the previous evening at the corner of Church Lane, when his attention was drawn to the defendant, whom curiosity led him to take to the office, where it was ascertained that she was a female. After the discovery had been made, 'Tom' became very communicative, and stated that she had been four years at sea, and was making her way to Hull, there to ship for Melbourne. On promising to leave the town without delay, she was discharged. 'Tom' smokes furiously, besides indulging in quids [tobacco] and nautical oaths, and her appearance corroborates her statement of long sea service. When discharged she left the court with a rolling gait.

The seagoing merchant navy had begun to introduce roles for women on board ships at around the time of this newspaper story, but their function was to serve as stewardesses to female passengers and children, and there were few posts. Slowly, the jobs for women at sea expanded but they were very restricted and included what would have been viewed as 'traditional' female roles in the late nineteenth and early twentieth centuries – positions such as cleaners, laundresses, nurses, waitresses, hairdressers, sales assistants, and cooks. These roles did not require women to undertake duties as seamen or work the ship, but they were registered as part of the *Central Index of Merchant Seamen* (1918–41) – see Chapter 4.

Some women became radio operators in the Second World War, but with a few exceptions it was not until after 1945 that women were permitted to take on other seagoing roles such as mariners, engineers, doctors, and deck officers. The first female master of a

British passenger liner was Sarah Breton, who took command of the P&O ship *Artemis* as recently as April 2010.

Uniforms

Prior to 1919, shipping companies used their own uniforms and there was little consistency between them for designating ranks. Officers usually wore a suit, and status was generally shown by a system of badges and sleeve stripes. The company emblem was often used as a cap badge. The uniform distinguished the roles of

The standard British merchant navy uniform for officers introduced in 1919. The uniform was blue, with sleeve stripes in gold. Senior engineers, surgeons, and pursers had one additional colour each to indicate their special-isation. The hashed areas in the illustration represents these colours – purple for engineers, red for surgeons, and white for pursers.

29

the various officers, encouraged discipline and respect among the crew, and helped to create a corporate identity. Many small companies did not provide uniforms.

In 1919, King George V showed his appreciation for the great courage shown by merchant seamen in the First World War by authorising a standard national uniform for officers belonging to the British merchant navy. This blue-coloured suit was not compulsory when introduced but it soon gained widespread acceptance despite some companies' initial reticence. The principal distinguishing feature is a diamond shape set into the sleeve rings. There is a white version for use in tropical climates, where the sleeve insignia are replaced by epaulettes to the same designs (see page 88). The cap badge is a plain anchor surrounded by oak leaves and surmounted by a Tudor crown. Some companies adopted the new distinctive sleeve rings, but continued to use their own company cap badges.

Before and after 1919, there was no national uniform for seamen or other non-officers employed in the merchant navy. For most of its history, non-officers in the merchant service would have been expected to provide their own clothes; it is mainly from the twentieth century onwards that passenger ship companies began to provide a distinctive pattern of clothes suited to their employee's role and the company's image.

Family Photographs of Merchant Navy Personnel

Discussion of uniforms inevitably leads to questions about how to interpret photographs of merchant navy crews. A detailed account of this subject is beyond the scope of this book, but the following tips may help you:

- Victorian photographs often show merchant seamen or officers in unremarkable clothes that give no clues to their seafaring life. There is no pattern of facial hair that can be taken to identify nautical men.
- If the subject is wearing a cap with a badge, you may be able to identify the shipping company. Unfortunately, there is no published guide to merchant navy cap badges, but illustrated books about shipping companies may help you, or you may be able to identify the badge on the internet if you can describe it suitably. The website http://flagspot.net displays an online

*The standard merchant navy officer's cap badge from 1919 onwards (left)
compared with that for a Royal Navy commissioned officer (right). Although
there can be much variation in presentation, key differences are that: (1) the
anchor is fouled with a chain in the RN badge, and (2) the RN crown is similar
to that of the modern crown jewels, whereas the merchant navy crown is of more
ancient 'pointed' style.*

collection of house flags which often show the same emblems
as cap badges. Books which identify company logos used on
ships' flags and funnels include *Ships and the Sea* by E.C.
Talbot-Booth (Sampson Low, Marston & Co, various editions
beginning 1936).
- Cap badges help to distinguish merchant navy and Royal
Navy officers (see image). However, some merchant seamen
became officers in the Royal Naval Reserve (RNR) and so
wore a navy cap badge when they were deployed, especially
in the world wars (see Chapter 7). RNR officers have distinctive 'wiggling' sleeve stripes.
- The uniform for Royal Navy seamen is usually easy to identify, but if you are uncertain examine the upper arms for naval
badges. These can be indistinct in black and white photographs because they were made of red material on a blue
background. A lens will often pick them out.
- A man wearing a peaked cap is not necessarily a captain,
because other officers also wore them; he may not even be an
officer because peaked caps were common headware for
seafaring men, regardless of rank. Also note that non-
maritime professions wear caps (e.g. army officers).
- In the late nineteenth and early twentieth centuries crews of

The man on the right wears the standard uniform of a second officer in the merchant navy. Note cap badge and sleeve rings with a diamond. The man on the left does not wear the standard uniform – the zigzags on his sleeve suggest he may be a chief steward as some companies used this convention.

large yachts often wore distinctive jerseys carrying the vessel's name in a cartouche across the chest. You can see an example in the image of the crew of the *Oimara* in Chapter 4.

- Details of a ship in the background may help narrow down the era – try to discern if the ship is of metal construction or wooden; check if rigging, sails, or funnels are visible; you may be able to see armaments; look at passengers' fashions.
- A photographer's address on the back of an image can suggest one port that the subject operated from, yet many merchant seamen travelled widely, and such information should be viewed as highly speculative unless other information supports it. Photographs were often taken far from home to

The distinctive 'rising sun' cap badge of P&O.

send back to a seaman's family to indicate he was safe and well.

- In Victorian and Edwardian times small children were commonly dressed as sailors and photographed. This does not indicate they came from families with maritime connections.
- Merchant seamen often had photographs taken to commemorate a specific event – such as completing an apprenticeship, earning a qualification, or captaining a first ship.

Health and Illness

Ships can be dangerous places: plunging wet decks increase the risk of falling overboard and drowning, or of slipping and breaking bones. In the days of sail, climbing high rigging meant that falls were likely to be fatal. Life on a sailing ship also carried the risk of hernias and strains from the frequent hauling and lifting required of the crew. There was the danger of being attacked by the enemy in wartime, or by pirates, and there are many means by which a ship itself can come to grief (see Chapter 6).

Going to sea carried infection risks, but before the late Victorian era the role of micro-organisms in causing disease was unknown. Doctors assumed that most diseases were caused by environmental conditions, diet, or human behaviour. The tightly packed community on board ship meant that transmissible diseases spread rapidly. In this regard, an infection that could be a major problem was dysentery – often known as the flux – which could run rife through a ship. In 1698, for example the *Robert and Elizabeth* sailed from Liverpool but before reaching its final destination of Philadelphia, forty-eight passengers and crew had died of the flux.

'Ship's fever' was a type of typhus transmitted between crewmembers by lice. Its initial symptoms are similar to influenza, but there is a characteristic rash and often an intolerance to light. As the disease takes hold, victims sink into a stupor, become delirious, and then die. A story about ship's fever in the *Liverpool Mercury* on 3 September 1847 illustrates its potentially devastating effects:

> The *Sir Henry Pottinger* sailed from Cork with 399 passengers, she reached the St Lawrence with 122 sick and 98 dead, and the *Virginius* and *John Munn*, which left Liverpool with 496 and 425 passengers, respectively, have arrived, the one with 158, and the other with 59 dead, while almost every soul of the survivors was hopelessly ill. Of the crew of the *Virginius* but 3 are left, the captain and officers having died with the rest.

The sexual appetites and frustrations of sailors trapped at sea for lengthy periods have long been the butt of ribald jokes. It's no wonder, then, that British ports have tended to attract prostitution. This, in turn, enabled the easy spread of sexually transmitted diseases and in particular, venereal disease or VD. There are two major forms: syphilis and gonorrhoea. Ironically, the crews returning from America with Columbus probably introduced syphilis to Europe.

Until penicillin was introduced in 1945, VD treatments were not very effective, and the disease spread because infected victims continued to have sex and passed it on to their sexual partners. The diagnosis was considered shameful, which made it difficult for sufferers to seek medical advice. The incidence of infection among

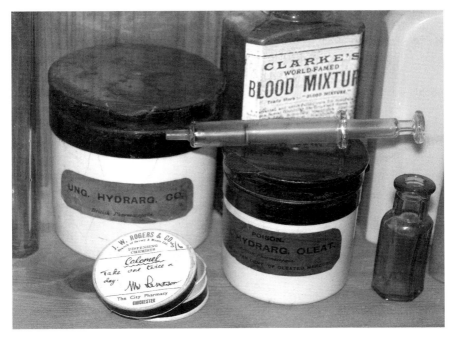

Early twentieth-century VD treatments.

merchant navy seamen is unknown, but it was a major problem: eighteenth-century logbooks from the Royal Navy often show lists of men afflicted with the condition. During the First World War there were approximately 417,000 hospital admissions for venereal diseases among UK military personnel.

VD was just one of a number of infections originating from far-flung places that sea travel enabled to spread. Cholera reached pandemic proportions in the nineteenth century. It seems to have started in India and spread around the globe in several waves of infection. It struck the UK mainland on four occasions: in 1831, 1848, 1853, and 1866 – where it lasted for about a year before subsiding. Seamen were especially at risk because they travelled to countries where the disease was active, and almost certainly brought it back to the UK on the four occasions when it broke out. Many British seamen died of cholera. James Robertson, a physician from Dunfermline, describes his treatment of the crew of a ship in January 1832 where one seamen, John Davidson, had already died of cholera:

Upon examining the crew of the sloop *Keith Douglas*, William Trotter, master, from Shields, I found the whole of the ship's company (three in number) in a state of bad health. The master and boy have been for three days past, annoyed with purging . . . They are to have quinine with soda, and a half grain mercurial pill every eight hours.

The mate was seized three days ago with looseness in his bowels, which continued until today, when vomiting, purging, cramp in the stomach, bowels and extremities, with general coldness, supervened. I immediately, on coming alongside, gave him 60 drops of laudanum [opium] in a wine glass full of brandy, which he vomited in a short time afterwards; then two grains opium, and to be repeated until the vomiting and purging subside. A large mustard poultice to be applied directly to the stomach and bowels, to lie on 40 or 60

A seaman fumigating a ship against cholera in 1850.

36

minutes, according to the degree of excitement it produces. One and a half grains of calomel [mercury] every hour; his bed placed on the cabin floor, and as large a fire to be put in the stove as can be done with safety to the ship.

Unfortunately, the mate soon died, but the captain and ship's boy recovered.

Once the world began to open up to oceangoing ships, seamen were exposed to more tropical diseases. Malaria became a particular risk for crews travelling to West Africa and southern Asia, and yellow fever was a notorious killer in both West Africa and the Caribbean. Both infections are transmitted by mosquitoes.

Notwithstanding infections, a far greater menace on long voyages was scurvy, which killed thousands of seafaring men every year in the eighteenth century. We do not know how many merchant navy seamen died, but figures from the eighteenth-century Royal Navy suggest more men were lost to scurvy than were killed by the enemy. Seamen were prone to this disease because shipboard rations for long voyages were deficient in vitamin C, and this caused the illness. Vitamin C is mainly derived from fresh fruit and vegetables, which do not keep for long at sea. Symptoms included bleeding gums, bad breath, a spotty complexion, and a very debilitating lethargy. Wounds did not heal and old ones re-opened; sufferers picked up infections easily, because scurvy damages the immune system. Eventually, men became too weak to take up their duties, and sometimes became delirious before they died.

Men in the merchant service had a reduced risk of scurvy compared to their naval counterparts because they spent less time at sea and their diet was often better. Nevertheless, crewmen on protracted foreign voyages could be badly affected. Although the navy introduced citrus juice as a preventative in 1799, it took until 1851 for legislation to force merchant navy shipowners to do the same and even then the law had to be strengthened in 1867 because of non-compliance. Since so many British seamen took lime juice, their American counterparts called them 'limeys'.

In 1867, a physician wrote in the *British Medical Journal*: 'Fever exists to a great extent in our coasting [ships], scurvy in our ocean-going ships, and venereal diseases in both.' Before the nature of these illnesses was properly understood, captains employed various means to reduce the risk of disease. Swabbing the decks with vinegar was favoured by some, as was fumigating the ship with burning sulphur. This latter probably helped reduce the rat population, but there were countless absurd and sometimes poisonous medicines peddled to seamen to treat or prevent illness – especially for scurvy, VD, and cholera. Many of these were even prescribed by doctors and, for VD and cholera at least, they frequently included the highly toxic substance mercury as the main ingredient.

Seamen commonly smoked tobacco in pipes and later cigarettes, as well as chewing it (tobacco quids) and snorting it up the nose (snuff). These days we understand tobacco's dangers, but before 1950 they were not recognised. In fact tobacco was often promoted as healthy. In the Royal Navy, men were even encouraged to buy it from their employer, who kept a large supply on all ships.

Finally, something must be said about seamen's long association with heavy drinking, an activity and a reputation at least partly fuelled by the ready availability of rum and beer on Royal Navy ships. The Victorian temperance movement often cited sailors as a particularly bad influence and made attempts to target them for reform – holding meetings in ports, and offering charitable support linked to zero tolerance of alcohol. In his widely read book, *The History of Drink*, James Samuelson insisted in 1878 that the problem drinkers in Victorian society were the lower classes, especially 'the vicious classes in the great seaports'. These seamen, 'whose chief employment is drinking', were in many cases foreigners serving on British ships, and were largely to blame for England's 'unenviable reputation for drunkenness amongst the nations of the world'.

Drunkenness was dangerous and taken very seriously when a crew was at sea because it stopped a man performing his duties, and this could endanger not only his own life, but that of others on board (e.g. by failing to keep watch properly). Crew agreements always stipulate that sobriety is mandatory.

By any of the above means, and more, seamen could die at sea. The official mechanisms for recording their deaths are discussed in Chapter 6.

Although large oceangoing passenger ships started carrying doctors in the nineteenth century, the majority of merchant ships did not. It was therefore down to the crew to organise medical treatment in many cases. After 1855, all ships leaving the UK for foreign waters were obliged by law to carry certain medical supplies; the type and amounts varied according to crew numbers, but the medication to be carried included items such as alum (for wounds), arrowroot (diarrhoea), rhubarb extracts (constipation), Dover's powder (fevers), lime juice (scurvy), mercury (infections such as VD), sulphur (skin infections, lice), opium (e.g. laudanum; for pain and to promote sleep), quinine (malaria), and zinc chloride disinfectant solution. There was also an agreed list of splints, bandages, trusses, tapes, lancets, needles, and so forth.

Charities and Retirement

Seamen had needs that were attended to by a large number of charities and other organisations, mostly originating in the Victorian era. In particular, there were organisations that provided these services:

- **Training** for young men to acquire seafaring skills. Especially in Victorian times this was seen as a way to create employment and take boys off the streets (see Chapter 4).
- **Disaster relief**. Food, care, clothing, and accommodation in the aftermath of a shipwreck (see Chapter 6).
- **Accommodation** and recreational facilities for seamen ashore while seeking employment. For example, the Southampton Sailor's Home provided overnight accommodation for twenty-six *Titanic* crewmen before they sailed in 1912.
- **Medical treatment** and hospitalisation for sick seamen. The Dreadnought Seamen's Hospital, for instance, was based originally on a ship in the Thames. Admission details survive from 1826 at the NMM (series DSH/1-46) and are indexed by series DSH/101-146.
- **Orphanages**. Although many orphans were adopted by relatives, if there was no close kin children could be left unsupported. In the nineteenth century, a series of orphanages sprang up close to major UK ports. Examples include the Hull Seamen's Orphan Asylum and the Sailors' Daughters' Home in Hampstead.
- **Christianity** and various moral messages (e.g. temperance) tailored to the needs of seamen. The Missions to Seamen started in England to provide a focus for Christian worship for seafarers, but soon expanded to operate all around the world.
- **Financial support and retirement accommodation** for impoverished ex-seamen and their families. For example, the

Royal Alfred Aged Merchant Seamen's Institution, Belvedere, Kent (opened 1867); the Aged Merchants Seamen's Home, Sunderland; the Destitute Sailors' Asylum, Dock Street, London (from 1827).

- **Trades unions** offered employment support, but surviving records are sparse. The Modern Records Centre has committee archives relating to the National Union of Seamen (NUS) dating to the late nineteenth century, but not membership records: www2.warwick.ac.uk/services/library/mrc/ subject_guides/family_history/seamen/. Some local archives may have NUS branch records carrying more details about certain members.

Port of London Society,
FOR
PROMOTING RELIGION AMONG SEAMEN.

On *TUESDAY, FEBRUARY* 13, 1821,
A PUBLIC MEETING OF LADIES & GENTLEMEN,
WHO
Feel an Interest in the Religious Instruction of Seamen,
WILL BE HELD
AT FREEMASONS' HALL, GREAT QUEEN-STREET,
Lincoln's Inn Fields.

THE RIGHT HONORABLE J. C. VILLIERS, M. P.
WILL TAKE THE CHAIR AT TWELVE O'CLOCK PRECISELY.

This Ticket will admit the Bearer and his Friends.

THE ABOVE REPRESENTS THE INTERIOR OF THE FLOATING CHAPEL.

The moral character and religious instruction of seamen was subject to considerable scrutiny by Christian groups in the nineteenth century.

Although some of these organisations were national (e.g. the NUS), the majority confined their activities to one area. Hence local archives are the best place to look for any surviving records, which may include details of those assisted, but don't forget that you may be able to use census returns to look at residents of many of the establishments supported by these charities. As the twentieth century advanced, many charities ceased to operate as the number of British seafarers dwindled, along with the charities' funds.

Before the twentieth century, it was difficult for most men to retire, because without regular income there were limited means of subsistence. Towards the end of his career a seaman might look for a less demanding role such as crewing a private yacht, or operating on ships closer to home. When they left the sea – through old age or injury – seamen often took up shore-based positions which required less physical effort. Some sought roles where they could use some of their nautical knowledge such as harbour officials or running a chandlery. A surprising number became pub landlords.

When a seaman or officer stopped working completely, a small national pension seems to have been available to some via the Merchant Seamen's Fund. When this fund was wound up, certain seamen or their dependants were still able to claim a pension. Payments were made from the War Office, irrespective of whether the seamen had seen war service or not, and some correspondence about individuals is preserved in the Marine Out-Letters at TNA (1851–1939; series MT4) although it can be hard to find. Before 1867, each volume is indexed.

Further details about individuals can be found in TNA series WO22: Royal Hospital Chelsea Returns of Payment of Army and Other Pensions. Seamen's pensions dating from 1842 are found among the others listed and include those for widows and children. They are in volumes arranged alphabetically by district, then date (e.g. Worcester 1842–52). There is no index, so it is best to search under likely location. The volumes for English districts are first, then those for Wales, Scotland, Ireland, and the colonies. For England, Wales, and Scotland, records stop at 1862. They describe the award of new pensions, the movement of pensioners to and from districts, deaths, and ineligibility for pension. Widows, for example, lost their pension if they remarried; children lost theirs on reaching the age of fourteen. There is also a single volume devoted to UK-wide merchant navy pensions for 1852–3 (WO22/208) which describes merchant seamen and their dependants who are no longer eligible for a pension through death or other cause.

Many retired seamen had to rely on savings, their family, or a charity to support them. This was often less of a concern for officers, who were better paid. A number of charities ran retirement homes for elderly merchant seamen or those who had been forced to stop working early due to injury, and men could apply to be admitted or to receive regular payments to support them in their own homes. There were a very large number of these organisations spread around the UK. Some unsupported and impoverished seamen finished their days in workhouses. Records for all of these local sources, if they have survived, should be sought in regional archives.

A good example of the charitable support available is Trinity House in London, an organisation that was responsible for, amongst other things, many of Britain's lighthouses. This organisation supported impoverished seafaring men or their families from all over the UK. A series of pension applications (1784–1854) are held at the London Metropolitan Archives (ref CLC/526/MS30218A-B), indexed in a volume on site entitled 'Trinity House Petitions'. The records often describe a mariner's career. For example, Margaret Wills of Poole applied for a pension after her

Retired mariners at the Royal Alfred Home for Aged Seamen, Belvedere, Kent in the 1880s. It cared for ex-merchant seamen who were 'old, destitute and friendless'.

husband, James, lost both of his hands when a cannon exploded on board his ship the *Vere* in 1842. James's entire shipboard career as a merchant seaman is listed from 1817. There is also a largely unindexed list of those who received financial support or accommodation from 1729 to 1995 (CLC/526/MS30218) and a separate, indexed, register of almspeople, 1845–1971 (CLC/526/MS30219).

The London Trinity House covered a large part of England and Wales, but some ports such as Hull and Newcastle had their own Trinity Houses, as did Scotland (Dundee and Leith). Local archive services may assist you in locating any similar records held for these organisations. Records for Leith, for example, are held by the National Archives of Scotland as series GD226.

The Old Age Pensions Act was passed in 1908, and enabled a meagre state pension to be paid to eligible people over seventy years of age. Gradually, state provision improved, yet shipping companies began to make provision for employees' pensions as well. For example, P&O had a pension scheme as early as 1915 and some of its staff records have survived at the NMM (P&O/81/1-52) as well as lists of retired personnel from 1880 (P&O/83/1) and of staff deaths from 1848, including those who had retired (P&O/88/3). On investigation, you may find that similar records have survived for other shipping companies.

Chapter 3

FINDING AND FOLLOWING A SHIP

It is a vital aspect of research into any seaman's career to identify the ships that he served on, but an extra dimension is added if you can find out what they looked like, the details of the voyages for which he was engaged, and the ship's ultimate fate. Family historians may also have many other reasons for wanting to trace a ship – maybe you have an ancestor who was a passenger on a particular vessel, who owned ships, or even built them.

Before discussing some of the major sources available to assist you, it is important to understand the three principal methods by which ships are differentiated from one another in records – that is to say via their name, official registration number, and tonnage.

Ships' Names and Numbers

Merchant ships or 'merchantmen' have commonly been named after people: either simple forenames (*Elizabeth, Diana*), famous individuals (*Princess Caroline, William Wilberforce*), or mythical figures (*Queen of the Isles, Athena*). Female names tend to predominate. Sometimes human names reflect the owner's identity (*James Manlaws, Henry and Anne, The Three Brothers*). Another common theme is to use words that reflect the desirable attributes of a ship – its speed, grace, role – or the owner's approach to business, and examples include *Velocity, Ranger, Enterprise, Patience*. Geography is also used for inspiration (*Gulf of Paria, Chichester, Humber Pride*), as well as animals or plants that are associated with the water or are considered motivating (*Otter, Cygnet, Mayflower, Tiger*). Finally, there are names that were chosen probably because they were memorable and hence many of these are more obscure. With so much competition for trade in the merchant service, anything that

WHITE STAR LINE ⬢ R·M·S· MAJESTIC

56,621 TONS

THE WORLD'S
LARGEST LINER

The Majestic in 1924; shipping companies often chose inspiring names to attract passengers.

helped customers remember your vessel was an advantage; examples here include *Black Dwarf*, *The Staff of Life*, and *The Nameless*. Some names seem ill-chosen – one wonders how many people would have chosen to go to sea in the *Casket*, or to invest in the *Miser*.

Contemporary ship names are often inspired by marketing, particularly in the case of cruise ships, which may need to reflect a company identity or create an attractive image of a holiday afloat – e.g. *Sovereign of the Seas*. In this light, the modern Italian cruise company Costa may not have helped to attract custom by naming one of its liners the *Costa Fortuna*.

In 1786, the Merchant Shipping Act required all British ships over 15 tons to be registered at a named port (see below) and to have their name and port displayed prominently. Importantly, this act forbade the re-naming of ships. This is fortunate, because tracing ships that have been re-named is not always easy, as many investigators discover when tracing ships after 1875, when re-naming was permitted.

Note that certain prefixes have been applied to British merchant ships to indicate their role or their propulsion system (e.g. RMS *Titanic*). They have not always been used consistently, but common examples include:

- MS or MV – motor ship or motor vessel
- MY – motor yacht
- RMS – royal mail ship
- RV – research vessel
- SS – steamship
- SV – sailing vessel
- TS – training ship.

An official numbering system for ships began in 1855. A unique number was given to every British-registered ship and kept throughout the ship's life. The numbers were never re-used, even after a vessel was scrapped or lost. Many sources quote the official number, where it is often abbreviated to 'ON', but not all of them reveal the vessel's name. So a method of decoding the official number is sometimes required. Fortunately, the Crew List Index Project (CLIP) cross-indexes all numbers awarded between 1855 and 1955 with the ship's name at www.crewlist.org.uk/data /vesselsnum.php.

Ships' Tonnage

Tonnage is mainly used historically as a measure of the ship's capacity to carry cargo, not its weight. The word 'tonnage' is supposedly derived from the number of large casks of wine – or tuns – that a ship could carry, each holding 252 gallons.

You will find some variation in the quoted value for a ship's tonnage between sources, particularly before the mid-Victorian era, so it is not always a reliable means for differentiating ships with the same name. Some captains and others may have mis-remembered the figure when asked to recall it. In addition, the preferred method of calculating tonnage has changed with time and the different methods produce different results; the methods used have varied between countries as well. Sometimes the tonnage was rounded up, and sometimes rounded down, and the extent of rounding up varied. It is also true that different values could be quoted for different purposes. For most of the eighteenth century, up to three different tonnages could be quoted per ship – the owner manipulating the figure he declared depending on whether he was selling his ship, paying port duties, or filling it full of cargo.

In the eighteenth century the main formula used for calculating a ship's tonnage was:

$$\text{tonnage} = \frac{(\text{length} - \tfrac{3}{5}\,\text{breadth}) \times \text{breadth} \times \tfrac{1}{2}\,\text{breadth}}{94}$$

The universal adoption of this method within the British Empire explains why quoted tonnages often include a number of 94ths. For example, in 1823, George Light of Shoreham expressed the tonnage of his ship the *Hiram* as 'one hundred and twenty-five tons and 17/94 parts of a ton'.

In about 1850, a change was made when 100 cubic feet of enclosed space was determined to be equal to 1 ton. This gross register tonnage (GRT) was the usual measure quoted for merchant ships until the late twentieth century. Nett register tonnage included deductions for spaces where passengers and cargo could not be accommodated (e.g. engine room).

As its name suggests, displacement tonnage is the volume of seawater the ship displaces when it is afloat and represents its actual weight. This figure is usually used for military ships.

Tracing a Ship

There are a variety of information sources to help you, but the ones you select will be determined by what you want to find out, the era in question, and how easily you can access the resource. To help you decide, these factors are highlighted in the descriptions of each resource that follow, but the basic sources for ships can be grouped into two categories:

The ship as property	The ship and its voyages
Who owned it, and where was it based?	*Where did it sail, and how often?*
What did the ship look like?	*Was it involved in any notable incidents?*
Who built it, and when?	*Did it carry cargo or passengers?*
1. *Lloyd's Register of Shipping*	1. Newspapers
2. *Mercantile Navy List*	2. *Lloyd's List*
3. Ship registration documents	3. Ships' charges and fees (see Chapter 5)
4. Ship plans, photo libraries, survey reports	4. Shipwreck records (see Chapter 6)
5. Websites about ships	5. Shipping company records (see Chapter 1)

Lloyd's Register of Shipping

- Coverage: 1764 to present day.
- Access: free full text via Google Books for 1770 to 1870 at http://books.google.com. Many later Victorian editions at http://openlibrary.org/. Holdings in UK libraries and archives are described at www.lr.org/Images/17%20location%20of%20regs%20new_tcm155-173528.pdf.
- Information provided includes: ship's master and owner, tonnage, age, place of build, port of registry.

Lloyd's Register is published annually, and should usually be your first port of call for any research involving a named ship. The vessels are mainly UK and British colonial, but there are some foreign-owned ships. The content and format has varied over the years, but ships are always listed in alphabetical order. Until 1834, the *Register* only included ships assessed by Lloyd's, so many vessels were omitted. Between 1834 and 1837, Lloyd's attempted to include all British-registered ships over 50 tons, regardless of whether they assessed them, but this was abandoned after 1838. From about 1875 onwards the *Register* lists every British vessel over 100 tons, whether surveyed by Lloyd's or not, although vessels under 100 tons were still included if Lloyd's did assess them.

There are many abbreviations throughout the *Register*, and you should consult the introduction to decode them. In terms of Lloyd's assessments, the early registers used the five vowels to describe the integrity of the hull, with 'A' being the highest quality. Masts and rigging were originally designated G (good), M (middling), or B (bad), but after 1776 the numbers 1, 2, and 3 were used instead. Accordingly, the best class of ship was described as 'A1', being a vessel of lowest risk to financial backers, underwriters, merchants sending cargo, and passengers.

During the eighteenth century, some shipowners began to feel that Lloyd's assessment methods could be too harsh – or at least inconsistent – and that the organisation was becoming too powerful in determining the fate of shipping businesses. A poor assessment meant no cargo, no investment, and an expensive refit. It all boiled over in 1799, when a group of dissatisfied men clubbed together to prepare their own assessment register. This was called *The New Register of Shipping by a Society of Merchants, Ship-Owners and Underwriters*, or more simply – because of its distinctive cover – The Red Book. It was published separately to *Lloyd's Register*, and the two books existed side by side. They have some overlap in content, but until the estrangement was healed in 1834, you must consult both sources.

When the shipping companies and Lloyd's settled their differences, they agreed a standard method of assessment. The new *Lloyd's Register* which resulted had standardised assessment rules. From 1834, the letters A, Æ, E and I described a ship's structural quality. Those designated as 'A' or 'Æ' were both first-class ships but differed largely in their age and the quality of the timber used. Ships rated as 'E' were unsuitable for transporting goods that would be damaged by seawater as they were prone to leakiness. Rather worryingly, class 'I' ships were described as only suitable for short voyages. The numbers 1 or 2 were added to these letters to signify the quality of the storage conditions for cargo – '1' being 'sufficient' and '2' being simply 'deficient'. So 'A1' was still the top level of assessment to which shipping companies aspired. This was later changed to '100 A1' for vessels with steel hulls.

Since 1834, the *Register* has been published on 1 July each year so, for example, the 1856 edition continued in force until June 1857, when it was succeeded by the 1857 edition. There can be two slightly different versions of each *Register* in circulation for any given year because some were kept regularly updated or 'posted' with new information sent out by Lloyd's to paste into the original. This new information might include the loss of a vessel, for instance.

From 1854, some ships were marked in the *Register* with a cross ✠. This meant that the ship was 'built under special survey' or more explicitly that the construction of the ship was supervised by *Lloyd's Register* surveyors – a fact that was used by owners to promote their ships' seaworthiness.

As the *Register* has evolved it has been split into different sections. As early as 1802, a collection of new ships notified to Lloyd's too late to make the main body of the text was included as a separate supplement at the back, and this continued in

No.	Ships.	Masters.	Tons.	BUILD.		Owners.	Port belonging to	Destined Voyage.	Classification.	
				Where.	When.				No. Years first assigned.	Character for Hull&Stores.
201	Margaretha I. B.	G Freese	59	Ppnbg	1836 3 mo	Capt.	Rhader -fatha	Glr. Hmbro'	7	A 1 36
2	Margarets I.B	Bg Brunton	88	Sndrld	1817	Maitland	Aberdn	Sld. Coaster	—	Æ 1 36
3	—	Sw T. Cook	81 139	ᴺᴰ.&Ts Anstru Irp.36	ds 32 1825	Srprs 36 W.Nicoll	Dundee	Dun. Rigɩ	—	Æ 1 36
4	—	Sr T. Milne C.34	152 142	Frrypt	1828	M'Gavin	Dundee	DunDantzic	—	Æ 1 2
5	—	Bg P Wallace C 31 RLoudon	168	Grngm	1826	Henry& S	Boness	Lon. Liv.Petersbg	8	Æ 1 E 1 35 6
6	Margaretta I.B.	Sr G.ːCooper	90 78	Fowey Drp.36	1828	Knill &Co	London	Lon.Lisbon	10	A 1 36
7	—	Sp T. Davis	59 54	Abrysɩ ᴺᴰ. 33	1814 Irp.36	Davies &	Abstwh	Abs.Coaster	—	Æ 1 36
8	—	Sr N. Henry pt I B.	123 115	Nwcstl O.&Lh	1832 ptRP	J. Nelson plk,len.&Sr	Nwcastl prs 37	Nwc.Coastr	5	A 1 3
9	Margarita	Sw M'nkman	184	Blythe	1835	Watson &	London	Lon. Cadiz	11	A 1 35
210	Margery	Sr D.Pringle	82 61	Dndee	1837 4 mo	A. Spence	Dundee	Dun.Nwcstl	8	A 1 4
1	—	Wheatley	318				Nwcastl			
2	Maria s.31,s. M.35	S	501	P.E.Isl BB.P.	1826 Hk & S.	Zalueta &	Cadiz	LonRioJan.	—	E 1 35
3	—	R. Adam	142				London			

Part of a page from the 1838 edition of Lloyd's Register.

subsequent editions. These vessels are grouped by the first letter of the ship's name but are not in alphabetical order, so if you can't find a vessel listed for a particular year, look there. Before 1802, these 'last minute' additions were listed at the end of every separate alphabetical section – e.g. a new ship called *Wayfarer* would be added out of alphabetical order at the end of the 'W' section.

Previous names for ships were given in the *Register* for the first twenty years of its publication. They were cited in the main text, next to the ship's current name. This practice ceased when name-changing became illegal, but from 1875 onwards there is a helpful supplement at the back revealing ships' former names. Steam and sail began to be listed in separate sections in 1886, so if you only know the ship's name and not much more about it, you do need to check both sections. From 1900, the *Register* recorded shipowners' addresses with a list of all the vessels they owned as an appendix.

If you cannot find a sizeable ship listed in *Lloyd's Register* before 1875, it may be because it was not assessed by Lloyd's. You should also note that *Lloyd's Register* has always tended to focus on foreign-going vessels rather than ships confined to the British coast (home trade vessels or 'coasters'), and that even before confining its attentions to ships over 100 tons, it generally listed few vessels of less than 50 tons.

An important spin-off publication is *Lloyd's Register of Yachts*. This was introduced in 1878 and continued until 1980, recording similar details to the main register for the world's larger yachts – whether used for pleasure or racing. Listing was on a purely voluntary basis but it is reasonably comprehensive.

There have also been a number of competitor registers to Lloyd's which occasionally list British ships. They include the *Registre Veritas* (French, from 1829) and the *Record of American and Foreign Shipping* (from 1871).

Lloyd's List

- Coverage: from 1741 to present day (some issues before 1779 have not survived).
- Access: not available online. Holders include Caird Library at the NMM (Greenwich); Guildhall Library (London); Merseyside Maritime Archives and Library (Liverpool); Southampton Central Library; National Library of Scotland.

- Information provided includes: ship location, movements, news, captain, and 'casualties'.

Whereas *Lloyd's Register* was published annually, *Lloyd's List* was originally issued weekly but soon became a daily publication. *Lloyd's List* recorded what is generally known as shipping intelligence – news about the fortunes and progress of individual vessels. It is a major source for investigating the loss of a ship (see Chapter 6). It was principally concerned with international voyages, rather than UK coastal trade, but includes ships from all around the British Empire.

Although the format of the publication has varied considerably with time, in every era there are sections concerned with reporting the most recent known location of a ship. These state the date that vessels arrived or departed a port, and when they were seen at sea (sightings) or communicated with another vessel (speakings). Starting in Victorian times, the *List* noted all the passenger ships about to depart from major UK ports for foreign destinations, together with their captains' names. From 1854, the *List* also included advertisements for these ships, showing departure dates and destinations, but often extra information of value such as fares and the name of the shipping company.

The more relevant section of the *List* to family historians is that providing updates about the fate of individual ships – usually news of a grim nature. This is often termed the 'casualties' section, although it is not always labelled as such in the *List* itself. It includes notices of collisions, damage, capture during war, wrecks, losses, salvage operations, and the fate of crews and cargo. Note that ships' masters are usually mentioned, but not always. When captains' names are given, the surname only is provided with no initial, and it is cited immediately after the name of the ship. Here are two typical entries from different eras:

23rd February 1776. The *Grace*, Elder, belonging to London, foundered about eight leagues to the southward of Cape St Antonio. The captain was 13 days in his boat, and arrived at St George's Key, in Honduras, about the middle of November. He took his passage in the *Lion*, Capt Lions, for London. The *Grace* was loaded with sugar and rum from the north side of Jamaica, bound to London.

4th Oct 1842. Sunderland – The *Return*, Young, from Shields to Leith, ran on shore upon Bamborough Sands last night, having been in contact with the *Apollo* of Montrose, but was assisted off and brought in here this morning, with much damage to hull, and loss of anchor, sails etc.

If you find news about a ship in a particular issue, you should check the next few editions as well because the *List* often provides serial updates on a vessel's condition: for example, a ship is reported first as running aground, then the cargo is rescued, then the ship is refloated or abandoned.

Lloyd's List has three main indexes, which run sequentially:

- **1741 to 1838**. The index for the casualty news for most editions is available free at www.cityoflondon.gov.uk/lloydslist/. The database allows you to search by ship's name, captain's surname, date, and the location of an incident. It sometimes provides a brief summary of the event concerned, but you need to order a copy of the original page from one of the archives that holds it to see the complete description.
- **1838 to 1927**. The *List* incorporated its own annual index, which is available separately on microfilm at many of the archives that hold copies of the *List* itself. It is an alphabetical listing by ship's name, with the captain's name appended where known, and refers the reader to a particular issue.
- **1927 to 1975**. A conventional index was abandoned in favour of regularly updated 'voyage record cards' for every individual ship. These are filed by ship's name, and are only available at the Guildhall Library, London. You must give prior notice if you wish to view them.

Lloyd's List is still published daily and the modern version can be seen at www.lloydslist.com.

Mercantile Navy List

- Coverage: 1850 to 1983 (except 1941–6). From 1977 known as *Official List of British Registered Ships*.
- Access: some editions 1850–67 via Google Books http:// books.google.com. Some editions 1868–1907 at http://

Official No.	Name of Ship and Port of Registry.	Rig.	Where built.	When built.	International Code Signal (if any).	Registered Tonnage.	Name and Address of Sole Registered Owner, or of Managing Owner when there are more Owners than One.
68118	County of Perth, Glasgow	S.	Whiteinch	1874	N.C.F.T	1626	R. & J. Craig, 136, Hope Street, Glasgow.
49116	County of Pictou, Glasgow	S.	New Glasgow, N.S.	1865	H.F.K.M	683	Geo. McKenzie, New Glasgow, Pictou, N.S.
60334	County of Stirling, Glasgow	S.	Kelvinhaugh	1868		999	R. & J. Craig, 136, Hope Street, Glasgow.
7043	Couranto, Workington	Bk.	Workington	1849	J.R.H.M	353	Frederick Payne Puckle, 87, Great Tower St., City, London.
56494	Courier, Aberystwith	Bg.	Sunderland	1866	H.P.F.V	283	John Francis, Glanywern, Borth, Cardigansh.
32609	Courier, Auckland, N.Z.	K.	Brisbane	1853	Q.W.S.T	31	Hugh Falconer Anderson, Auckland, N.Z.
9528	Courier, Guernsey	Bk.	Jersey	1849	K.H.R.D	320	Geo. F. Carrington, Guernsey.
63490	Courier, Guernsey	Cr.	Guernsey	1873		39	Chas. Le Page, St. Andrew's, Guernsey.
47084	Courier, Hong Kong	Bk.	Jersey	1863	V.M.D.T	386	Hong Kong, Singapore, & Borneo Trading Co, Hong Kong.
45113	Courier, Hull	Sk.	Rye	1863		50	John Baker, Hull.
54908	Courier, Leith	Sr.	Hempstead, Gloucestersh.	1866	L.W.P.B	98	Wm. Millar, Crail, Fife.
53963	Courier, Melbourne	K.	Williamstown	1866	N.H.G.J	34	Richard Grice & T. J. Sumner, Melbourne.
21665	Courier, Milford	Sk.	Hakin, Pemb.	1859	J.V.R.S	22	Alexander McKay, Milford, Pembrokeshire.
60293	Courier, Montrose	Sr.	Montrose	1869	V.L.D.S	128	Jonathan Knight, Padstow.
46843	Courier, Newport	Bg.	Pr. Ed. Is.	1863	N.M.K.V	210	David Price, Newport, Monmouth.
22679	Courier, Portsmouth	Cr.	Jersey	1858	P.H.L.K	17	Wm. Treadgold, Portsea, Hants.
25792	Courier, Whitehaven	Bg.	Whitehaven	1845	H.V.Q.W	115	William Robinson, Whitehaven.
51149	Courtenay, London	Bg.	Topsham, Dev.	1867	N.C.K.L	185	Thos. Goldfinch, Whitstable.
20737	Cousins, Exeter	Sp.	Topsham, Dev.	1858	Q.S.G.L	31	George Ellet, Exmouth, Devon.
31748	Cousins, Melbourne	Sr.	Tasmania	1850		17	Mrs. C. Isaacs, Emerald Hill, Melbourne.
64232	Cousins, Montego Bay	Sp.	Montego Bay	1874		20	Joseph Phillips, Montego Bay, Jamaica.
		Sp.				44	William Forrest, jun., Blackburn, Lancashire.

Part of a page from the Mercantile Navy List of 1875.

collections.mun.ca/. More extensive paper collections at e.g. Southampton Central Library and Caird Library at the NMM.
- Information provided includes: official number, port of registry, town where built, tonnage, name and address of principal owner.

The *Mercantile Navy List* (*MNL*) was an annual register of British ships produced by the Registrar General of Shipping and Seamen. Although it includes less detail than *Lloyd's Register of Shipping*, it does have one significant advantage: since registration was compulsory, after 1855 the *MNL* records *all* British ships of any description over a quarter of a ton. So a large number of ships too small to come to the attention of *Lloyd's Register* are included, and every ship is listed, regardless of whether Lloyd's assessed it or not, or whether it was a foreign-going ship or not. The *MNL* includes most ships registered in Empire and Commonwealth countries as well. Before 1855, it only records registered steam vessels.

From 1875 onwards, an appendix to the *MNL* recorded vessels listed in the previous edition that were no longer in existence for any reason. This includes causes such as wrecked, stranded, broken up, lost, missing, condemned, and sold to a foreign owner. A date is also given, which marks the date that the ship's British registration was closed.

Another advantage of the *MNL* is that the date recorded for the vessel's building is usually the year of completion as a seagoing vessel, rather than the earlier dates of laying down the keel, official launch, or finishing the hull. The year of completion is usually the same as the year of the ship's registration which can help you find the official ship's registration document (see next section). For motor and steam vessels, the *MNL* explicitly records the year of registration.

The disadvantages of the *MNL* over *Lloyd's Register* are that the amount of information recorded for each ship is much smaller – for example, it does not record captains' names, builders' names, engine details, or the dates of significant repairs. So it is usually a second choice after *Lloyd's Register*.

National Ship Registration

- Coverage: 1786 onwards for London, but mainly 1814 onwards for rest of UK.

- Access: hard copies available at TNA in series BT107 (1786–1854), BT108 (1855–89), and BT110 (1890 onwards) for England and Wales. Some originals are held at regional archives. The National Archives of Scotland holds some Scottish registrations, but others are at local archive offices.
- Information provided includes: detailed description of ship, when and where built, names of owners, list of successive captains, fate of vessel.

The Merchant Shipping Act of 1786 compelled all owners of ships over 15 tons to register their vessels at a designated home port. A list of all registered ships was kept centrally for England and Wales for 1786 to 1793 (BT6/191-3) by port, although these lists yield little information of genealogical value as the main details recorded were simply the ship's name and tonnage. The total number of ships registered in 1786 was surprisingly large, at 9,559.

However, a detailed registration form also had to be completed for each ship. Officials sent copies of them to the Registrar of Shipping in London, where a central annual archive was compiled, and these are now held at TNA. Regrettably, the records for ports outside London before 1814 have been lost, as well as some odd subsequent years, but these gaps at TNA can be overcome if county archives still hold the originals – it is worth checking. Note that Liverpool has a particularly good collection of registration documents which pre-date all other ports, extending as far back as 1739. These can be seen at Merseyside Maritime Museum Archives.

The registration document identifies the type of ship (e.g. a cutter) and then provides a description – tonnage, width, length, and rig, the number of decks, and whether it carried a figurehead. Just as importantly, there are often unique details about a family or individual. The owner's occupation is usually recorded, for example, and in identifying successive owners and captains it is common to find evidence to support family relationships – a man and his brother-in-law owning a ship between them, a father bequeathing a ship to his daughter, and so on. As property, British ships had to be divided into sixty-four after 1825, so you will typically find owners expressing their share in sixty-fourths.

Registration documents also describe a ship's origin, sometimes in surprising detail. For example, Captain George Light's descendants would probably be fascinated to learn that his small brigantine, the *Hiram*, which he registered at Shoreham, Sussex, in

1823 was actually built 3,000 miles away in New Brunswick, Canada, in 1811.

At TNA, all ship registrations are filed by year of registration in bound volumes: BT107 and BT108 are jointly indexed by name of vessel in BT111. This index is crude – it will tell you the port and year(s) of registration, and the vessels' tonnage – but it is not uncommon to find ships missing from the index despite them being registered. There are a number of 'runs' of the BT111 index which cover various dates and they do overlap, so consult the finding aid in the relevant red file 'paper catalogues' at TNA because you may have to look in more than one part of it.

Before 1826, the registrations volumes are separated into 'London', 'Western Ports' (Southern England plus Wales), and 'Northern Ports' (remainder of England plus Scotland). After 1826, the volumes are simply arranged alphabetically by name of port. So to find registrations for Exeter in 1816, you would look in BT107/156 (Western Ports: A–E), but for Exeter in 1860 you should look in BT108/64 (Ports A–G).

If you do not have a ship's name but hope to recognise it by other means (e.g. name of owner), you may consider looking through all the registrations within a defined time period for a given port to find it. This is time consuming but achievable for a short run of BT107 or BT108 records from a small port like, say, Milford in Wales, but not realistic for the largest ports such as Liverpool: there are simply too many records. Even for the smaller ports, you must bear in mind that registration did not take place annually, and that records were filed by year of most recent registration, which you will not know at the beginning of you search. If you were interested, for example, in Captain John Carter's unnamed ship from Plymouth which you know was wrecked in 1832, you could start at the 1832 Plymouth registrations (BT107/212) but would have to look back through several years of them until you found his ship *The Brothers*, which was first registered seven years before, in 1825 (BT107/180).

A change in home port usually triggered re-registration, as did any major repairs that significantly affected the dimensions of the ship, but it was not required when a different captain was appointed, and a successive list of ship's masters is found on the back of each document. When re-registration occurred, a note was made on the previous registration document to show where to look for the new one – e.g. 'registered *de novo* Hartlepool May 1838'.

Note that for series BT108 only (1855–89), any transfers of owner-ship are noted on the document using a code number and year (e.g. 5549 6/65). The details are in series BT109. In the example given, you would look for transaction number 5549 in BT109 for June 1865. It shows the sale of the ship *Richibucto* by Charles Mozley of Aberdeen to William Wood, a merchant, residing at 6, Great Winchester Street, London.

Ships registered after 1889 are found in BT110, but in a complete reversal of previous practice they are grouped together under the decade when registration *ceased* (e.g. when a ship was scrapped or lost). Within each decade, the individual records are filed alphabet-ically by ship's name, regardless of port of registry. For example, BT110/8 is every ship whose registration ceased in 1891–1900 with names beginning with 'B' through to 'Baz-'. Hence, BT110/8/1 is the *Bacchante*, BT110/8/2 is the *Bacchus*, and so forth. However, TNA has now started to index online every individual BT110 regis-tration record by ship's name, and at the time of writing has reached about 1930. This means that you can use TNA's Catalogue or the advanced search in the Discovery service at www.nation-alarchives.gov.uk/catalogue to search for a ship's registration document by inputting the ship's name and limiting the search to series code BT110. You still need to visit TNA to see the original document.

Particularly before the 1860s, registration documents can be the only source that records a vessel's ultimate fate. It may do no more than record that the ship was 'scrapped' or 'lost' and give a date, but sometimes there is a more detailed account or even a note of the edition of *Lloyd's List* to look at. For example, Captain George Traill of Newcastle lost his ship *Queen of the Isles* on the rocks off the coast of Cadiz on 2 April 1837. We know this only because the registration document records that the British consul wrote to the port authorities at Newcastle to inform them.

Registration papers kept at the National Archives of Scotland are indexed by ship's name on its website, www.nas.gov.uk.

Ship Pictures, Plans, and Surveys

Most UK maritime archives have collections of ship photographs and paintings (see Chapter 8). Three of them have particularly extensive image collections: Merseyside Maritime Museum Archives, the Caird Library at the NMM, and the Southampton

Archive Service. However, if you know the home port for a ship, it is worth contacting a more local archive or museum to see if any images have survived. It was common for captains and owners to commission portraits of their ships in the nineteenth century.

You can search the internet for pictures of a named ship, but there are free sites with quite extensive collections of images, including the Allen Collection at www.benjidog.co.uk and the websites www.photoship.co.uk and www.wrecksite.eu.

Newspapers can be a source of photographs, but they are often of poor quality until the late twentieth century. In the Victorian era, newspapers began to include quite extensive line drawings to illustrate their stories, and many of these images are of ships; their quality is often far superior to the photographs of the time. The *Illustrated London News* is a particularly good example of a periodical that includes many illustrations of named ships dating from 1842 onwards. Unfortunately, the online version is not available for personal subscription, but many libraries and archives do subscribe and some subscription genealogy websites include part of the collection.

If the vessel concerned was owned by a shipping company rather than privately owned, then books describing the history of the company are usually filled with illustrations. All the maritime archives have sizeable collections of books about companies.

A number of websites hold histories of individual ships or details about their voyages, including www.theshipslist.com and www.mightyseas.co.uk (mainly north-west England), but often a general search of the internet will yield a surprising amount of information.

Mariner's Mirror is a periodical dating from 1911. Over the years it has included a broad range of feature articles about named ships from all around the UK – the greater proportion of them featuring vessels before the twentieth century. They often include detailed descriptions as well as accounts of the ship's history.

There are various places in the UK where you might obtain the original building plan for a ship. These design documents are known as ship plans. There are often collections in local archives based in shipbuilding ports such as Glasgow, Newcastle, and Dundee. If you know the name of the shipbuilder, you can sometimes determine whether the company's archives have survived, and where they are held, by consulting the National Register of Archives: www.nationalarchives.gov.uk/nra/default.asp.

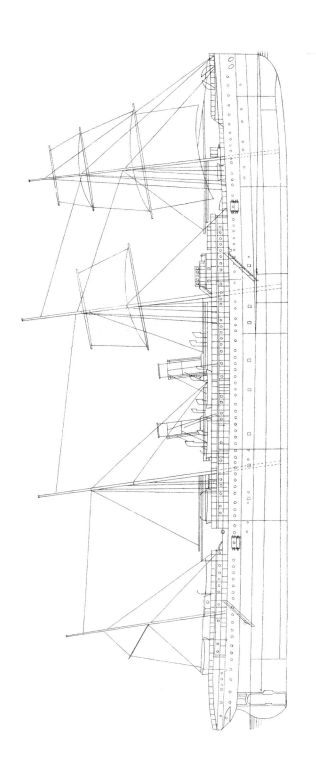

Ship plans reveal the detailed structure of a vessel.

The NMM in Greenwich houses the biggest collection of ship plans in the world. Over one million plans are available, but not all of them have been catalogued yet. The collection includes many of the original survey plans and detailed reports that *Lloyd's Register* undertook when assessing vessels, and these date from 1833 to 1964 (series GB0064). To enquire whether the ship you are interested in has a plan or survey report available, write to: Historic Photographs and Ship Plans Section, National Maritime Museum, Greenwich, London SE10 9NF. You must cite the name of the ship, its launch date, and identify the builder. Merseyside Maritime Museum Archives also has an extensive holding of ship plans dating from the late eighteenth century, while *Lloyd's Register* headquarters in London has a large collection of plans for named yachts dating from 1880.

Websites About Ships

Finally, there are many websites that describe the histories of a selection of ships – including their origins, owners, voyages, captains, and fates. Databases of this nature will never be comprehensive, but some recommended ones are:
- Palmer List of Merchant Vessels: www.geocities.com/ mppraetorius/
- The Ships List: www.theshipslist.com/
- Miramar Ship Index: www.miramarshipindex.org.nz (subscription required)
- Ship Index: http://shipindex.org (subscription required).

Chapter 4

TRACING SEAMEN AND NON-OFFICERS

Seamen, mariners, sailors, or ratings are non-officers with seafaring skills. The seaman has often had a hard life – not least because the behaviour of weather, sea, and ship can be unpredictable. The role could be physically demanding, but mentally challenging as well: keeping one's concentration while working with the same group of colleagues, and often on the same tasks, day after day, and being away from home for prolonged periods. In the era of sail, a seaman would be expected to work the ship, maintain her, and help load and unload cargo. Seamen worked shifts known as 'watches' (see Chapter 2).

The development of steam-powered ships created new jobs

Some of the crew of RMS Macedonia *in 1922 – seamen and non-seamen, men and women.*

within the crew – working in the engine room, for example – and as passenger ships evolved, roles developed that catered to the needs of the public. Some of these roles are discussed in Chapter 2, but many required no nautical skills. The guidance on tracing ancestors in the present chapter applies to all seagoing crewmembers, whether seamen or not.

Apart from apprenticeship records (see below) there is, unfortunately, very little chance of tracing the career of merchant seamen before 1835 if they were not captains. Some musters survive before 1835 but they are few and far between. Records of privateers and press gang protection registers offer a glimmer of hope (see Chapter 7), as do wills. Many seafaring men registered their wills via the Prerogative Court of Canterbury (PCC) so this collection of wills on TNA's website is worth searching, although note that the seamen's wills also listed there belong to Royal Navy crewmen, not merchant navy.

There are some sources for tracing seamen after 1850 which are described in other chapters. These include sources describing Royal Navy reservists (from 1860) or action in the world wars (see Chapter 7), awards and deaths at sea (Chapter 6), crewmen supported by charities (Chapter 2), and personnel described in shipping company records (Chapter 1).

Merchant Navy or Royal Navy?

This is an important question which can be vexing if a man is described in records as a 'seaman' or 'sailor' without further qualification.

If a man is described simply as a 'seaman' without further information, it is not possible to be sure if he served with the merchant navy or the Royal Navy, yet the term 'mariner' usually indicates a role in the merchant service. (Although be careful not to confuse 'mariner' with 'marine', indicating a member of the Royal Marines). If a ship's name is mentioned, note that navy records commonly omit the 'HMS' prefix before a vessel's name, so do not assume that its absence indicates a merchant ship. Furthermore, it has been common for navy men to be identified in formal records by their name and ship together, similar to a soldier and his regiment (e.g. 'Edward Carter of His Majesty's Ship *Unicorn*' or 'John White, able seaman, *Victory*'). This is something that merchant seamen have been less inclined to do because they generally moved from ship to ship more frequently. If a document mentions a seaman's captain, navy men typically cite being 'under the command of Captain X', whereas in the merchant service a captain is invariably referred to as the ship's master.

The term 'sailor' has tended to be used by those without a nautical background; in the twentieth century the Royal Navy often used the term 'rating' to refer to seamen.

Censuses

A number of subscription websites include indexed census returns for 1841 to 1911, among them www.ancestry.co.uk, www.findmy past.co.uk, and www.thegenealogist.co.uk. Records from the census can help you trace a merchant seaman, but it's important to understand their limitations. The 1841 census only included seamen who were on land at the time, so most were not recorded. However, you can still trace wives and children ashore.

From 1851 onwards (1861 for Scotland) seamen on ships docked at a UK port during the census were included as well as those at sea in territorial waters. Despite this, a large number of seamen went unrecorded in 1851, but accuracy progressively improved in subsequent censuses, when citizens at sea beyond territorial waters were also supposed to be documented. The census information about ships' crews is filed at the end of the records for the port concerned, except for 1861, when ships were all grouped together in one big section of their own. You will not know where a merchant navy ancestor was during a census, so keep an open mind when searching. Don't confine your search to where you expect them to be: their ship could be anywhere. When searching the census for seamen on land, you should consider that they may be in temporary accommodation pending a voyage, or in a care facility/hospital if elderly or injured. These establishments will not necessarily be close to the man's original home (see Chapter 2).

The census returns usually tell you the person's rank, age, marital status, place of birth, the name of the ship, and the captain's name. If on board ship, from 1861 more information is documented about the vessel: there is a standard page after the list of crew, recording the vessel's type (e.g. steamship), tonnage, home port, and official number, among other information. Don't forget to look for this second page.

Apprentices and Trainees

In the nineteenth century, most seamen were trained on the job. If he had little seagoing experience, a new recruit would join a ship as a young teenager with the rank of 'boy'. He would be given menial tasks such as cleaning, stowing cargo, and assisting with food preparation, but as time allowed he would also be taught the elements of seamanship by the rest of the crew.

Since medieval times there has also been the opportunity to take up an apprenticeship. This was a formal arrangement by which a young man agreed to undertake employment over a set period of time in exchange for training to reach a certain proficiency. Collections of indexed apprenticeship records can often be found in local record offices and may include apprentice seamen.

TNA has registers of duties paid on apprenticeship indentures: series IR1 dates from 1710 to 1811 and the unindexed records can be downloaded via DocumentsOnline's digital microfilm initiative (eventually to be replaced by the Discovery service). The Society of Genealogists' index for 1710–74 is available via www.findmy past.co.uk (subscription needed). The registers record apprentices' names, the date of indentures, father's name (until 1752), and the name, address, and trade of the employer. Merchant navy employers were often identified by the term 'marin'. TNA's online Research Guide to apprenticeships offers more information.

London Metropolitan Archives has a collection of apprentice indentures for seamen, who petitioned Trinity House for aid (reference CLC/526/MS30218D, mostly 1810–51). The Society of Genealogists has a private set of original apprentice indentures called the Crisp and Clench Collection, which may be worth searching for seamen. There are also some nineteenth-century apprenticeship records for various towns among records of the Boards of Customs and Excise – type 'apprentice' into TNA's Catalogue or the advanced search in the Discovery service and limit the search to series CUST.

Many apprenticeship records have not survived, and in many cases formal records may never have existed, particularly when a boy was apprenticed to a family member.

The Marine Society was a charity founded in 1756 and focused on training impoverished boys 'of good character' to supply the Royal Navy and merchant service with well-trained seamen. Those who opted for the merchant service started an apprenticeship with the society and completed it at sea with an employer. From 1862 to 1939 the Marine Society's training ship was called the *Warspite*. Merchant service training records survive at the NMM, but note that most boys came from London:

- Boys received and discharged 1786–1874 (series MSY/K)
- Register of admissions 1825–1958 (MSY/L and indexed MSY/M)
- Apprentices sent to merchant ships 1769–1950 (MSY/Q with some indexes in MSY/R).

Apart from apprenticeships, some organisations offered specialised training to young men seeking a life at sea. In the seventeenth century, Christ's Hospital Mathematical School was probably the first institution to offer formal training in navigation. Many of its students became officers in the Royal Navy or merchant service, and records of those studying can be found at the Guildhall Library, London, dating back to the 1670s. A number of other schools with similar aims were also established.

Crew of the SS War Leopard *in 1919. Two apprentice seamen sit at the front; the bosun sits centre wearing a cap, and next to him, holding a pith helmet, is the carpenter. In the back row wearing a hat is the lamp trimmer, and at far left the gunner. The rest are seamen.*

The law changed in 1823 to encourage more seagoing apprentice-ships. Captains of ships in excess of 80 tons were bound to take at least one apprentice. This was enforced by port authorities. TNA holds an alphabetical index of these apprentices between 1824 and 1953 as series BT150, with volumes arranged in date order. BT150/1-14 deals with London apprentices before 1880, while BT150/15-46 covers non-London ports ('outports') for the same period. From 1880 onwards apprentices from London and outports are in the same volume (BT150/47-57). These records provide the name of apprentice, age, the starting date for an indenture and its duration, and the name of the employing master. From about 1830 onwards, the name of the ship served on and its port is usually given.

Where no ship name is provided in BT150, it may be possible to deduce it by tracing the career of the master (see Chapter 5). Once you have identified a merchant navy apprentice in BT150 it may be possible to obtain a copy of his original indentures. Unfortunately, only every fifth year of records was preserved, but you can see these in BT151.

Note that apprentices often appear in the various registrations of merchant seamen described below as well.

The training ship Worcester *on the Thames at Greenhithe.*

In the nineteenth and twentieth centuries a whole series of organisations grew up to train young men for a life in the merchant navy, sometimes via an apprenticeship. Most of these schools were initially based in floating ex-navy ships, such as the *Arethusa* on the Thames, and were designated training ships (TS). Many later moved to land-based premises. For example, TS *Formidable* commenced training in Bristol in 1869, but became Portishead Nautical School in 1906. Some schools specialised in training officers, who were often referred to as cadets, but others trained seamen instead or as well. HMS *Conway* (established Liverpool 1859), HMS *Worcester* (London, 1863), and the Nautical School at Pangbourne (1917) were the three principal sites that focused on officer training.

Although officer training schools recruited young men on a fee-paying basis, those that catered for seamen were mostly government funded or charities. Many state-sponsored schools sought to provide safety and a future career for homeless, orphaned, destitute, or neglected boys (e.g. TS *Grampian* in Belfast). Others aimed explicitly to reform young men who exhibited antisocial behaviour by exposing them to a highly disciplined environment. These 'reformatory boys' were accommodated in facilities such as TS *Akbar* in Liverpool (established 1856). Some of the charitable institutions would only take 'poor boys of good character' (e.g. TS *Mercury* at Southampton). Many shipping companies had their own separate training programmes.

From 1872 onwards the *Mercantile Navy List* (see Chapter 3) details all state or charitable training establishments for merchant seamen. Local or national archive services may have more details of these organisations' activities including, in some cases, registers of admissions. For example, Merseyside Maritime Museum Archives has records of trainees for HMS *Conway* from 1859, and records of TS *Akbar* are held by Lancashire Record Office.

Certificates of Discharge

These documents may survive among family papers, but there is no central archive of them. However, if you do have one, they are most valuable and provide a shortcut to the information which you can otherwise obtain only by looking in the sources described in the rest of this chapter.

From 1854 onwards, merchant seamen were issued with a certificate of character and discharge when a voyage ended. They record

(E-1) CERTIFICATE OF DISCHARGE.

For Seaman discharged before a Shipping Master.

Name of Ship.	Official Number	Port of Registry.
Martha Pope	14283	Liverpool

Registered Tonnage.	Description of Voyage or Employment.
141	W. Indies

Name of Seaman	Capacity.
John Wightman	17166

Place of Birth: Dumfries

Date of Birth: 1815

Port of Discharge: Malta

Date of Entry.	Date of Discharge.	Place of Discharge.
Apl 12/59	Mch 14/60	London

✠ Certify that the above particulars are correct and that the above Seaman was discharged accordingly.

Dated this 17 day of April 1860

For Signature of Seaman see back.

Signed _____ Master of the Ship.

_____ Shipping Master.

NOTE.—One of these Certificates must be filled up and delivered to every Seaman who is discharged whenever the discharge takes place before a Shipping Master.
Printed by Authority of the Board of Trade.

SANCTIONED BY THE BOARD OF TRADE, MAY 1855, IN PURSUANCE OF 17 & 18 VICT. C.120.

MARINE DEPARTMENT.

(E-1) CERTIFICATE OF CHARACTER.

Character for ability in whatever capacity: Good

Character for Conduct: Good

✠ Certify the above to be a true Copy of so much of the Report of Character, made by the said Master on the termination of the said Voyage, as concerns the said Seaman.

Dated at London this 17 day of March 1860

Signed _____ Master of the Ship.

_____ Shipping Master.

For Signature of Seaman see back.

NOTE. Any Person who fraudulently forges or alters a Certificate of Character or makes use of one which does not belong to him may either be prosecuted for a Misdemeanour or may be summarily punished by a Penalty not exceeding £100 or imprisonment with hard labour not exceeding six months.

Printed by Authority of the Board of Trade.

SANCTIONED BY THE BOARD OF TRADE MAY 1855, IN PURSUANCE OF 17 & 18 VICT. C.120.

MARINE DEPARTMENT.

Certificate of character and discharge for John Wightman of Dumfries on leaving the ship Martha Pope in 1860, where he served as mate.

WATERS 3

Dis. A.

1939-43 Star
Ribbon Issued.

ISSUED BY
THE MINISTRY OF SHIPPING

4   WATERS

No. R 249413   C. R.

CONTINUOUS CERTI ## FICATE OF DISCHARGE,

with a Copy if
of the MASTER'S

desired by the Seaman
REPORT OF CHARACTER.

Name of Seaman, in full.	Date of Birth.
William WATERS	8th Dec 1926

Height.		Colour of		Complexion.
Feet.	Inches.	(1) Eyes. (2) Hair.		
6	0	(1) Blue (2) Brown	Fresh	

National Health Insurance.

Society.	Branch.	Membership No.
PRUDENTIAL.	SOUTHPORT	M 155YYO

Place of Birth and Nationality.	Certificate, if any.	
	Grade.	Number.
Pendeen, Cornwall Eng.	2nd Cl.	C/6397 C/7026

Tattoo or other Distinguishing Marks.

Signature of Seaman D. Waters

WATERS 7 ## CERTIFICATE
Or Certified Extract from List
and copy of Report of Character

OF DISCHARGE 8   WATERS

No.	Name of ship and official number, and tonnage.	Date and place of Engagement.	Discharge.	Rating.	Description of voyage.	Copy of Report of Character. For ability.	For general conduct.	Signature of (1) Master; and of (2) officer and official stamp.
	S.S. EMPIRE HEYWOOD REG. NUMBER 166212 PORT of REGISTRY DUNDEE GROSS TONNAGE 7029'94 REG. TONNAGE 4095'84	29.5.44 Cardiff	3-8-44 Cardiff	1st Radio Officer	7 H.T. of 15	VERY B 110 GOOD	VERY B 110 GOOD	(1) EXTRACT FROM CRS 3
8	S.S. INDIAN CITY O.N. 168867. BIDEFORD. G.T. 7079	6-9-44 Barry	24/5/45 B'head.	1st Radio Officer	8 Fgn.	VERY A 89 GOOD	VERY A 89 GOOD	(1) Ll CRS 3 (2) Co Tull [...] PENZANCE.
9	EMPIRE WOODLARK OFF. No. 168249 LONDON. N.T. 4448 I.H.P. 7000	3/4/45 FALMOUTH	20/4/45 MALDO N.	1st Radio Offic.	9 R.A.	VERY A 89 GOOD	VERY A 89 GOOD	(1) Ll CRS 3 (2) Co Tull [...] PENZANCE.
10	SAMTAMPA O.N. 169787. 7146 G.T. 4380 N.T. 2500 I.H.P.	MCHESTER	20/12/45 MCHESTER	1st Radio Officer	10 Fgn.	VERY A 89 GOOD	VERY A 89 GOOD	(1) Ll CRS 3 (2) Co Tull [...] PENZANCE.
11	S.S. SAMTAMPA O.N. 169787. 7146 Gross 4380 Net 2500 I.H.P.	24·1·46 Mchester.	L'pool	1st Radio Officer	11 Fgn.	VERY C.21 GOOD	VERY C.21 GOOD	(1) Meale Sherwell (2) J Mockly
12	S.S. SAMTAMPA O.N. 169787. 7146 Gross 4380 Net 2500 I.H.P.	JUL 25 1946 L'Pool	30 MAR 1947	1st RADIO OFFICER	12 Fgn.	VERY B 26 GOOD	VERY B 26 GOOD	(1) Meale Sherwell (2) G [...] 30 MAR 1947

* These columns are to be filled in at time of engagement.
† In Engineers' Books insert Horse Power. In Wireless Operators' Books insert gross tonnage and wireless classification of Ship.

R 249413

Pages from continuous certificate of discharge for William Walters, a radio officer in the Second World War.

the name of the ship, its official number, captain, home port, tonnage, and voyage details. The crewmember's name, signature, dates of service, rank, and place and date of birth are also recorded, as well as his 'character for ability' (professional skills) and 'character for conduct' (behaviour). It is unusual to find anyone whose character is not recorded as 'fair', 'good', or 'very good'. Presumably those who were given poor assessments were unlikely to keep their certificates. Collections of these certificates were used as references when seeking further employment.

In the twentieth century, a continuous certificate of discharge was introduced. This allowed seamen to record their entire careers in a single dark blue book. These books contain similar information to the above, but in addition usually contain a physical description, a photograph, and the seaman's home address. There may also be stamps in the book showing the issue of wartime medals.

National Registration

A series of six registration systems for seamen have been introduced since the first one was sanctioned by the Merchant Shipping Act of 1835. Each one met with administrative problems which led to its demise, and then it was replaced by another system. The value of registration to family historians is immense because the details enable a seaman's career to be mapped out, yet the way the records are organised can be confusing and some can be difficult to interpret. It is hoped that the descriptions below will clarify the situation for you.

The original registers are all at TNA, but the best means of access is now via the subscription website www.findmypast.co.uk which holds digitised copies of most of the documents – although the fifth register, described below, is not available from this source. The Find My Past records are fully indexed by name, and are linked to copies of the original documents so that you no longer need to visit TNA to see them. It also means you can search all of the registers simultaneously instead of one by one, thus avoiding the laborious process of hunting for individuals via the often challenging indexing quirks of the various series. Some library and archive services offer their users a free or subsidised access to Find My Past.

I have identified the registers and their associated indexes by their original TNA series codes (e.g. BT112), since Find My Past continues to use the same codes. However, note that you cannot search each register separately.

First and Second Registers

- Coverage: first register 1835–6; second register (1835–44).
- Access: first register BT120, second register BT112, index to registration numbers in second register, BT119. All three are

accessible via www.findmypast.co.uk (or on microfilm at TNA).

• Information provided includes: name, age, place of birth, rank (termed 'quality'), and ships served on

These registers were compiled using details from crew lists (see below). The first register lasted less than two years and is preserved as BT120. Due to the administrative burden it created, the first register was replaced by the second register (BT112), but data from the first register was copied across into it. In practice, this means that BT112 entries are usually more helpful than BT120, but either register may sometimes clarify details from the other. Each seaman was given a unique number which was used for both registers, but note that most entries for 1840 and 1841 are missing.

The index BT119 simply provides a man's name, registration number, and place of abode. For example: James Williams, 13146, Swansea.

The BT120 register will give you a man's name, age, rank, place of abode, and ship currently served on. For example: James Williams of Swansea was 24 when he registered in 1836, and was a mariner on board the *Elizabeth* of Liverpool. Men who ran away from their ship are marked 'Des' or 'Deserted'.

The BT112 register provides name, age, place of abode, rank, and details of voyages undertaken. This register was originally in two parts – 1835-40 and 1841-4 – so you will often find two records for each ancestor. After the crewman's name in BT112 come his voyage details in columns. His rank is indicated by abbreviations such as 'S' (seaman), 'AB' (able-bodied seaman), '1M' (first mate), and 'C' (captain'). The TNA website has a Research Guide entitled 'Abbreviations in Merchant Seamen's Records' which lists them all.

When voyage details are provided, the ship's name is usually given, with a numerical coding. This code indicates the year of sailing and the ship's port of registration (for coastal vessels) or UK port of return (for foreign voyages). UK ports were all given unique numbers to identify them according to an alphabetical index where 1 was Aberdeen, 2 Aberystwyth, 3 Aldborough and so on. The TNA Research Guide cited above lists them all.

For example, John Wilson from Hull's first registered voyage is written as 'S 6/36 52 205 *Arundel*'. This means he was a seaman ('S') serving in June 1836 ('6/36') on the *Arundel*, a ship based in Hull (port 52). The meaning of the number '205' is no longer understood.

His later voyages show that he moved on to other ships: the *Moscow*, *Phebus*, *Whim*, *Ruby* and so on.

If you want to search the microfilms of any of these records manually at TNA, you should consult the 'finding aids' for each of them because they are not always arranged in an entirely logical sequence. These aids are in one of the red file 'paper catalogues' for TNA users in the first floor reading room.

Register of Seamen's Tickets

- Coverage: 1845-54 (although few entries exist for 1849, 1850 and 1854).
- Access: the register is BT113, and its index is BT114. Both are accessible via www.findmypast.co.uk (or on microfilm at TNA).
- Information provided includes: place of birth and residence, age, date of birth, rank, time of first going to sea, physical description, and voyage details.

In this period, every seaman was given an official identity document called a 'ticket', without which he was unable to work. These tickets were numbered and seldom survive, but seamen's applications for them are preserved in register BT113 at TNA. These are the most useful of the Victorian registration systems because comprehensive pre-printed registers were used to record extensive details about individuals. The register has an alphabetical index at BT114 which provides name, place of birth and ticket number. Surnames with the same few initial letters are grouped together (e.g. Walcott, Walmsley, and Walsh, are on the same page). If you are not using Find My Past, locate your ancestor in BT114, then use the ticket number provided to locate him in BT113, which is arranged in numerical order. A typical BT113 entry is:

No. of register ticket	*341,705*
[name]	*John Jellows*
Born at	*Fairlight* in the county of *Sussex*
	19th day of *Mar 1825*
Capacity	*Seaman*
[physical description]	Height *5ft 7inch* Hair *Lt brown*
	Complexion *Sandy*
	Eyes *Grey* Marks *None*
First went to sea as	*Seaman* in the year *1847*

Has served in the Royal Navy	*No*
Has been in Foreign Service	*No*
When unemployed, resides at	*Fairlight*
Ticket issued at	*Rye 1st* day of *April 1847*
Age when ticketed	*22*
Can write	*No*

The subsequent voyage details are given as numerical codes similar to those used in the second register – i.e. rank, date and port number – but without naming the ship. For example, 'AB 919 117 7 48', refers to voyages by an able-bodied seaman ('AB') recorded in July 1848 ('7 48') in a ship registered at Caernarvon (port 117). This knowledge allows you to look through crew lists (see below) for Caernarvon in 1848 to try and identify the ship.

The ticket system has a number of quirks, which can be frustrating. For example, there are no entries in BT113 for ticket numbers beyond 546,000, even though these numbers may be provided by the BT114 index. You will also find some lamentably incomplete entries.

Third Register

- Coverage: 1853–7.
- Access: the register is BT116; there is no index. It is accessible via www.findmypast.co.uk (or on microfilm at TNA).
- Information provided includes: name, age, place of birth and voyage details..

Entries are arranged in rough alphabetical order, as in BT114 above, so locating an individual is relatively straightforward. Note that place of birth can be missing or vague (e.g. 'Scotland'). Voyage details generally include ships' names.

The third register was abandoned in 1857 without an immediate successor. This means that from this point until 1918 family historians must rely principally on censuses, crew lists, and family documents such as certificates of discharge. All of these are discussed elsewhere in this chapter. If your ancestor became an officer, there are additional resources available (see chapter 5).

Fourth Register (Central Index, Special Index, and Combined Index Registers)

- Coverage: 1918–41.
- Access: available online at www.findmypast.co.uk (subscription needed), on microfiche at TNA (series BT348-50), or see the originals at Southampton Archives Service www.southampton .gov.uk. BT364 is an additional register available at TNA only.
- Information provided includes: place and year of birth, ships served on, rank/role, discharge number, nationality. May include photograph, date and cause of death, physical description, and certificate number for officers.

In 1913, with war imminent, a national register of merchant seamen was begun once again, possibly with the objective of providing each crewmember with a merchant navy identity card. Unhappily, the documents relating to 1913–18 were all destroyed in 1969. The remaining register comprises a series of around one million cards of three types known as CR1 cards (series BT350), CR2 (BT348) and CR10 (BT349), with the latter generally providing most information. If possible, try to find more than one card type for your ancestor as they record different information. You will often find that more than one card of the *same* type has been completed for the same person.

Importantly, the register includes merchant navy employees of all kinds: not just seamen, but stewards, cooks, cleaners, firemen, barbers, and so forth. For the first time, women are included in the register in a variety of early roles as described in Chapter 2; this chapter also gives some of the abbreviations used for roles but the TNA Research Guide referred to under the second register, above, is also helpful.

By far the best way to access these records is via Find My Past's database because you can search all three card types online by name, year of birth, and place of birth. The quality of reproduction is also very good and you can download images of the cards to keep.

The microfiche images at TNA tend to be hazy and not easy to copy. If you do visit TNA then note that series BT349 and BT350 are presented alphabetically by surname, so are easy to use. However, the microfiche in BT348 are arranged in order of discharge number (DisA), this number usually being recorded in BT349 or BT350 cards, or on crew lists (see below). If the DisA number has a letter in front of it, this should be ignored when consulting BT348. The discharge number was so-called because crewmembers were only given short-term employment and could be discharged when each voyage ended. A unique DisA number for each person allowed them to be reliably identified by the authorities as they moved from ship to ship – it was the merchant navy equivalent of a service number.

The cards record other numbers besides the DisA. Some relate to health insurance or welfare benefits, but certain other numbers are important to further research:

- **Ship's official number (ON)**. Ships that the individual served on are sometimes identified by name, but often just by their official number (see Chapter 3) and the start date. Often these details are on the reverse of the card. You can identify the ships that official numbers refer to by putting the number into the CLIP website at www.crewlist.org.uk/data/vesselsnum.php or using the *Mercantile Navy List*.
- **RNR number**. If your ancestor joined the Royal Naval Reserve, this is their service number. See Chapter 6 for how to take this further.
- **B/T certificate**. This is the Board of Trade certificate for ship's

Registration systems and crew lists show the ethnic diversity amongst crews of British-registered ships. This picture was taken in 1905.

masters (captains), mates, and engineers and indicates that the individual was aiming to become an officer (see Chapter 5).

If you can't find an ancestor in this register he or she may have been on the cards covering 1913–18 that were destroyed. However, for some reason a selection of all three card types was removed from BT348-50 and used to create a new series, now known as BT364. These are now filed by DisA number only, although there is a short run of un-numbered cards filed alphabetically at the end. The DisA number can be obtained from crew lists (see below). BT364 is only available at TNA and is not on the Find My Past website. Some cards were also removed and inserted into the fifth register (see below). Finally, note that captains do not seem to be commonly recorded in the fourth register, for unknown reasons, and in this situation you should review the options set out in Chapter 5 to help you.

Fifth Register (Central Register)

- Coverage: compiled 1941–72 (but often includes service outside this period).
- Access: available at TNA only (series BT372 and 382).
- Information provided includes: place and date of birth, ships served on with dates of engagement, rank/role, DisA number, qualifications, and a note on character (VG = very good, G = good, etc.). BT372 includes details of next of kin, a physical description, and a photograph.

Some cards from the fourth register, above, were carried over into the fifth register if personnel were still active in 1941.

In BT382, a standard format called CRS10 was used to identify seamen and record their careers from 1941 onwards. The documents are arranged alphabetically by surname but in eight series which are not easy to define precisely. The contents and dates are broadly:

- European seamen, 1941–6. BT382/1–2022 and 3289.
- European seamen, 1946–72. BT382/2023–3078.
- Asiatic seamen (mostly Indian subcontinent), 1942–65. BT382/3079–3118.
- Asiatic seamen (mostly Indian subcontinent), 1966–72. BT382/3119–3137.

- Foreign seamen, including Chinese and Indian, 1941–72. Note anglicised spellings of names. BT382/3138–3231.
- Prisoners of war and internees, 1940–5. BT382/3232–3251.
- Merchant seamen serving on ships requisitioned by the navy, 1939–45. BT382/3252–3284.
- Deaths of seamen recorded for pension purposes, 1944–51. BT382/3285–3288.

CRS10 documents contain almost identical information to a continuous certificate of discharge booklet which may have survived as a family document (see above). Ships are named with their home ports and official numbers. Those marked 'F' are foreign-going vessels; those with an 'H' operated in home waters.

Within each series, records are ordered by surname so BT382/1 is Aadahl to Abbotts 1941–6, BT382/2 is Abbs to Abraham, and so on. You should identify which piece you need within a series and then order the original document at TNA. Note that because some documents may contain confidential information about persons still living there can be restrictions on what you can view, so consult TNA staff for advice.

To complicate matters slightly, a second series exists within the fifth register. This is BT372, often referred to as 'seamen's pouches' because the documents are presented in a wallet. They can incorporate cards from the fourth register, above, so service details may date back as far as 1913. There is often a photograph because the documents were used to issue identity cards.

Although filed by DisA number, the TNA website has an index to BT372 by name, date and place of birth. Simply type an ancestor's surname into the Catalogue, or the advanced search in the Discovery service, and restrict the search to series code BT372. If you return too many 'hits', add in a place of birth (e.g. Smith AND Bristol) or confine search dates to a narrow period within which your ancestor was born. The resulting citations provide a reference number to order the original papers from TNA (e.g. BT 372/334/149). Each document's title comprises the DisA number, name, date of birth and place of birth (e.g. R228109 SMITH G A 28/11/1909 BRISTOL). As with series BT382, there may be some restrictions on access.

Regrettably a large part of BT382 is missing, but there are still around 500,000 surviving records.

Musters, Crew Lists, and Agreements

As a result of the Act for the Relief of Disabled Seamen, from 1747 onwards merchant ship captains prepared a muster of their crews for every voyage. Unfortunately, few of them now exist, and those that do often fail to name every crewmember individually. However, they are worth checking if your ancestor operated from one of the few ports with a surviving collection as they may be your only source of information for seamen before 1835. You should check local record offices for survivals, but TNA keeps these pre-1835 musters in series BT98:

- Bristol 1831–
- Dartmouth 1770–
- Lancaster 1800–
- Liverpool 1772–
- Plymouth 1761–
- Shields and other northern ports 1747–
- Whitby 1800–

Crew Lists and Agreements

- Coverage: 1835 onwards.
- Access: various sources (see below).
- Information provided includes: name of each crewmember, rank, age, place of birth, previous ship served on, dates of service, when and where discharged, date and cause of death if applicable, voyage destinations.

From 1835, masters of ships were obliged to keep lists identifying every crewmember. They have survived because they were filed centrally by the Registrar General of Shipping and Seamen. Crew lists have a standard presentation. Initially, there were two common types: schedule C lists were written for each voyage to a foreign destination, whereas schedule D lists were composed twice yearly for all voyages in British waters over the previous six months. All crew lists compiled up to and including 1860 are held at TNA in series BT98. Note that they are filed under the ship's port of registry, not port of arrival or departure. To find them for the period 1835–56, simply type the name of the port into TNA's Catalogue, or the advanced search in the Discovery service, and restrict the search to

Crew lists exist for ships large and small. This photograph shows the entire crew of the private yacht Oimara, *many of them wearing jerseys embroidered with the yacht's name.*

series BT98. The crew lists are sorted by port name, then year, then alphabetically by ship's name. So BT98/140 is Aberdeen ships 1835–44 with names beginning with A or B; BT98/141 is the same port and era but ships beginning C or D, etc.

For 1857 onwards (from BT98/4759), crew lists at TNA are filed by ship's official number. If you have the ship's name the official number is obtainable from www.crewlist.org.uk/data/vesslesnum.php.

You must visit TNA to see the crew lists which are kept loose in boxes. They are not ordered by date or alphabetically, so you need to search an entire box to make sure you have all the records for a given ship, particularly since that there is usually more than one crew list per ship per year. Searching can therefore be a time-consuming task so allow enough time for your TNA visit. Some of the crew lists are damaged or have faint text; they can also be quite large documents. It is thus often easier to use a digital camera to record them, rather than the on-site photocopier.

Crew lists will help you construct a seaman's shipboard career. Of particular value is the column headed 'Ship in which he last served'. This can be used to find the crew list for the seaman's previous ship and so trace a career back in time. Analysis of other crewmembers' names may reveal family connections – particularly in the nineteenth century – because officers often selected relatives to serve with them. Knowledge of regular voyages can explain geographical mysteries in your family's history such as how a man from Exeter ever married a woman from Canada. Crew lists quite commonly record precious details that are not recorded elsewhere. For example, descendants of boatswain Samuel Lowery from Belfast may not realise that he died of yellow fever in Antigua in 1851, while on board the *Sobraon*.

Crew agreements or articles were introduced from 1845 and describe crewmembers' terms of employment. These are filed with crew lists. Schedule A agreements were for foreign-going ships, and schedule B for ships operating in UK waters. They describe the crew's duties and the standard of behaviour expected.

From 1861 onwards, crew lists and agreements are no longer held together in one place because no British institution could be found with sufficient space to accommodate them all. The table below summarises where to look:

Years	Held by
1835–56	TNA, series BT98. All ships except famous ships (see below). Indexed in TNA's Catalogue/Discovery service by port of registry and year of voyage.
1857–60	TNA, series BT98. All ships except famous ships (see below). Indexed in TNA's Catalogue/Discovery service by official number.
1835–1999	TNA, series BT100. All records for famous ships such as *Cutty Sark*. Search by ship's name in TNA's Catalogue/Discovery service.
1861–1938	TNA, series BT99. A random 10 per cent sample indexed by ship's official number in TNA's Catalogue/Discovery service, and by ship's name after 1924.
1861, 1862, 1865, 1875, 1885, 1895, 1905, 1915, 1925, 1935, 1955, 1965	Caird Library, NMM. All ships for these years, apart from what TNA has in BT99 or BT100. Ships and crewmembers for 1915 are gradually being indexed by name in TNA's

	Catalogue/Discovery service as series BT400 even though records are at NMM.
1867–1913	National Archives of Scotland, all Scottish ships.
1863–1938	Maritime History Archive, Canada. Holds everything not held by above archives: about 70 per cent of the total. Indexed by official number on their website www.mun.ca/mha.
1939–50	TNA series BT380 and BT381. All ships except famous ships (see BT100, above). Search by ship's official number in the Catalogue/Discovery service. BT387 contains crew lists for foreign Allied ships requisitioned or chartered by Britain.
1951–76	Maritime History Archive, Canada, as above.

To complicate matters further – if that were possible – some regional archives retained a small selection of crew lists for local ports from 1863 to 1913. Fortunately, the Maritime History Archive (MHA) website identifies these. Follow the link to online crew lists at www.mun.ca/mha, then type the official number of the ship you are looking for into the search engine. This will tell you if the MHA holds the crew list, or if a UK regional archive holds it. Note that this index does not include the holdings of TNA and the NMM. You can order copies of crew lists from the MHA by post or email for a fee.

If you are unfamiliar with crew lists, the MHA provides a very helpful online tutorial describing their purpose, appearance, and how they can be used for research at www.mun.ca/mha/mlc/index.php.

Crew List Shortcuts

There are a number of places where crew lists have already been indexed by crewmembers' names. Perhaps the most ambitious is the plan by the MHA to index every crewmember on every crew list for 1881 to form a 'maritime census' to accompany the conventional British census of the same year. This database can be searched free at www.mun.ca/mha/1881/crews1881.php. TNA has also indexed its 10 per cent holding of 1881 and 1891 crew lists by name. Search the Catalogue of Discovery Service by surname, restricting to Series BT99.

Other online indexes include:

- The subscription website Find My Past includes some indexed crew lists dating from the 1860s onwards.
- If you have Welsh ancestors, there are two websites that index many 1861 to 1900 crew lists: www.swanseamariners.org.uk and www.cardiffmariners.org.uk.
- Family History Indexes has indexed personnel on crew lists from 1851 for all of Wales, Scotland, and Ireland, and for Cornwall in England. These indexes are available for purchase from their website, www.fhindexes.co.uk.
- The MHA has indexed a random 1 per cent sample of its British crew lists and this is available to buy on CD: www.mun.ca/mha/holdings/names/index.php.
- Some nineteenth-century crew lists for Guernsey are indexed at http://history.foote-family.com/maritime/index.php.
- Some websites that record passenger lists, also record crewmembers. For ships sailing to Australia, for example, try http://mariners.records.nsw.gov.au/.
- Certain local record offices have in-house indexes to their holdings.

Crew lists were printed in black ink and kept on board ship for submission once voyages were complete. From time to time, you may come across a crew list printed in red ink, which was the shore-based copy. Red copies usually indicate that the ship was lost, taking the original black crew list with it, so the red copy was substituted.

Ships' Logs

Logs were kept by the vessel's master, and a few survive in private hands or regional archives, dating back to the eighteenth century in some cases. However, from 1850 captains had to keep a log of certain events on board their ship by law, including births, deaths, serious illness, and breaches of discipline. Often these logs, which were in a standardised format, are included in collections of crew lists and agreements, but many have been lost. TNA has a collection dating from 1857 to 1972 as series BT165, which is particularly rich for the period 1902–19. They are indexed in TNA's Catalogue, or via the advanced search in the Discovery service, by ship's name and official number. Sometimes logs provide extra details above what was required by law, but they do not record a day-by-day account of life on board.

Documenting a Career

Maritime professions tend to run in families and it is difficult enough remembering one individual's merchant navy career, let alone a whole series of people. A good method to adopt is to construct a summary table for each man, otherwise you can quickly lose your way. Suitable headings are suggested in the example below, which is part of the career of Henry Wills from Dorset:

Years	Vessel (captain)	Rank	Vessel description	Home Port (owner)	Destinations
1812–18	**Mary** (his father, Henry Wills)	Boy	Pilot boat	Poole (his father, Henry Wills)	Poole and local coast
1819	**Enterprize** (Capt. J. Pimer)	Ordinary seaman	Brig, 156 tons	Poole (Thos Colborne)	Newfoundland, Mediterranean
1820	**David** (Capt. R. Miller)	Ordinary seaman	Brig, 130 tons	Poole (Slade & Co.)	Newfoundland, Mediterranean
1821	**Otter** (Capt. H. Green)	2nd mate	Schooner, 81 tons	Poole (Cox & Slade)	Newfoundland, Mediterranean
1822	**Marnhall** (Capt. J. White)	1st mate	Brig, 104 tons	Poole (J. White)	Newfoundland, Mediterranean
1823–5	**Pomona**	Master	Brig, 97 tons	Poole (Slade, Cox & Slade)	Oporto, Danzig, Newfoundland

You should record the fine details and your sources elsewhere, but a summary like this helps you keep track of your research and to present it coherently. After 1855, it's a good idea to incorporate ships' official numbers into column 4 (see Chapter 3).

Chapter 5

CAPTAINS AND OTHER OFFICERS

It is generally easier to trace merchant navy officers than seamen because officers' activities were more likely to be recorded in contemporary records. For captains in particular this provides plenty of opportunity to research an ancestor, but does present a significant problem: where to begin?

The present chapter discusses the certification of captains and mates, which became compulsory in the 1850s, and for engineering officers from 1861. Early location of a copy of a certificate and application form will save you a lot of time. Otherwise, the best place to start is determined by what you already know, what you want to find out, and the era. So consider the following points:

- Almost all resources describing seamen's careers – such as national registrations and crew lists – identify officers as well (see Chapter 4). Also see Chapter 4 for facilities that specialised in training officers.
- If you know your ancestor's ship or home port, then the information sources in Chapter 3 will help you, but only if he was the captain. They include *Lloyd's List* and *Lloyd's Register*, and ship registration documents. These sources are all vitally important for captains.
- Perhaps you know your ancestor was an officer because he received an award, died at sea, or was involved in a shipwreck. In which case, see Chapter 6.
- If your ancestor officer was active after 1862, and particularly if he served in either world war, you should check records for the Royal Naval Reserve (Chapter 7). If you know he served in the merchant service in either world war, perhaps because you have medals or discharge papers, then refer to the same chapter.

- Records of shipping companies (Chapter 1) may provide information about officers.
- An officer active before 1815 might have gone to sea in a privateer or have been granted a protection against being taken by a press gang (see Chapter 7).

Captains and Mates

Captains of merchant ships were known as the ship's master or sometimes its commander. The informal term 'skipper' is used to

In hot climates officers could wear the white form of the standard merchant navy uniform. This photograph shows a group on board SS Abbassieh *in 1935.*

refer to masters of small vessels, but is also commonly adopted by seamen and pleasure boat owners without a master's qualification.

The mate was the second-in-command and principally responsible for the crew, cargo, and safety. If there was more than one mate, they were numbered for seniority, so that the most senior was first or chief mate, the next most senior was second mate and so on. During the twentieth century, the term 'mate' gradually became less popular and the chain of command below captain has often been chief officer, then first officer, second officer, etc. (although some ships do not have both chief officer and first officer).

Before certification of officers became compulsory, it was left to shipowners to decide when a man was experienced enough to command a ship. In the nineteenth century it was common for a man to be appointed to his first post as ship's master in his twenties. Typically, this first command might be on a 'coaster' – a ship that sailed in UK home waters within sight of land – or on a vessel with which the new captain was already familiar because he had served on it as mate.

While some captains commanded only a small number of vessels for their entire careers, others progressed rapidly through a long list of ships. Coastal vessels tended to be more secure positions with greater chance of ongoing employment and less risk of the ship being lost; they also attracted men who did not want to be away from their families for long periods. Oceangoing ships were generally larger vessels with bigger crews; they carried more cargo or passengers, and could make longer voyages, so their owners paid higher wages.

It is easier to trace captains after they were required to be certificated in the mid-nineteenth century. Both before that time, and afterwards, *Lloyd's Register, Lloyd's List,* and ship registration documents are vital sources that extend back to the eighteenth century. See Chapter 3 for more information on all of these.

Ships' Charges and Fees

Captains of merchant ships had to make various compulsory payments whenever the vessel entered a port. These might include docking fees, pilotage charges, port duties, and so forth. While records for most of these have not survived, there are some early sources of this nature that can help you trace the career of a captain by telling you the name of the ships he commanded and where he was at a particular point in time. They are described below.

Port Records

- Coverage: 1565–1799 (many years missing).
- Access: for England and Wales in series E190 available at TNA, filed by port name and then year. No indexes to ships by name and no online access. Similar records for Scotland can be found at the National Archives of Scotland as series E71, E72, and E504.
- Information provided includes: name of captain, ship, cargo, date of payment of duty, merchant who owned the cargo, and destination and/or port of origin.

Customs officers in ports kept records of merchant ship activity to ensure that duties were paid on goods. Their books were sent to the Exchequer annually and acted as a kind of end-of-year report. Unfortunately, the surviving port books represent only a proportion of those originally written: many have been destroyed. There are no port books for London for the entire eighteenth century, for example. Some ports stopped compiling records after about 1750.

Surviving port books do not include all the trade for the period concerned: ships' captains and owners were keen to dodge customs duties when they could. Smuggling was rife during the whole period that port books were in operation, and this led, for example, to cargoes being landed at night some distance from a port so that duties were avoided. It is also probable that some ships' arrivals were not recorded because crooked customs officials took bribes or kept the payments themselves.

Port records are divided into two or three different books for each year. Coastal vessels transporting cargo between UK ports are usually in a standalone book; they received a certificate exempting them from customs duty. Foreign trade is recorded in two additional books, but sometimes one; they describe the movement of ships and the duties paid for importing and exporting goods. You will usually have to look at all of the books for any given year to find a particular captain. The records for smaller ports were usually overseen by officials at a nearby larger port, so at TNA the records for Hartlepool, for example, are indexed with Newcastle.

Early books are mostly in Latin, but English predominates from the seventeenth century. If you know, or suspect, that a certain ship or captain operated from a particular port, then port books can provide proof and add extra detail. The entry for a small ship carrying one type of cargo is short – typically two lines only –

whereas entries for ships carrying a mixed cargo can be wonderfully detailed. A typical entry from a 1756 coastal trade book for Plymouth reads as follows:

21st Sep
In the *Joseph & Elizabeth* of Emsworth, Joseph Prousting Mr, [from] Chichester, for Richard Andrews Ind, 110 quarts of wheat. Certificate dated 15th instant.

The captain's name is always given immediately after the name of the ship and 'Mr' means 'master'. The certificate mentioned was issued at Emsworth to prove these were British goods (and so exempt from tax) belonging to a merchant Richard Andrews who was 'Ind' or 'indigenous' – i.e. a British subject.

A more detailed overseas trade entry from London in 1567:

14–15th Nov
Mary Anne of London (80), John Bonner [master]; [arriving from] Bordeaux.
Cuthbert Bucle: 50 tuns Gascony wine, net 45 tuns 135s; 4 tuns vinegar £9 6s 8d (14 Nov).
Hugh Offley: 6 tuns Gascony wine, net 5 tuns 15s (15 Nov).
Randal Hankin: 3½ tuns Gascony wine, net 3 tuns 1 hhd 9s 9d; ½ tun vinegar, 1 tun turpentine, 40 cwt brazil, 20 pcs resin £81 3s 4d.

This entry shows imports for the merchants listed by name, and the monetary values are the duties that they each had to pay. Measures are always abbreviated; here 'hhd' is hogshead, 'pcs' is pieces, and 'cwt' is hundredweight. The '80' after the ship's name is its tonnage.

The main value of port books lies in tracing the movements and cargoes of individual ships, identifying the commands of captains, and the trading activities of merchants. The books contain a wealth of abbreviations, which can take some getting used to – particularly the shortened form of many archaic measures. Occasionally port books add unexpected facts, such as the tonnage of the ship, the ship type (e.g. brig), details about the captain (e.g. his origins), or even refer to passengers. The type and frequency of this extra information depends on the era and the diligence of the recorder.

Sixpence Duty and the Seamen's Fund

- Coverage: 1725–1830 (Thames); 1800–20 and 1832–51 (Exeter); 1834 (whole UK).
- Access: for the Thames, series ADM68/194–217 at TNA; the only index is a short run by captain's surname in ADM68/219 covering 1745–52. Exeter is series BT167/38–40. The UK-wide listing for 1834 is ADM68/218.
- Information provided includes: name of captain, ship, tonnage, home port, last port visited, crew numbers.

Officials known as 'Receivers of the Duty of Sixpence' collected a tax from ships' captains to fund the medical treatment of seamen at Greenwich Hospital. In the eighteenth century, they paid sixpence per month for every seaman on board. This Sixpence Duty later became the Seamen's Fund. Payments were made irregularly – whenever a receiver caught up with the ship concerned – but records were kept and the captain was given a receipt, so it was not too difficult to identify payments owing. Most accounts have been

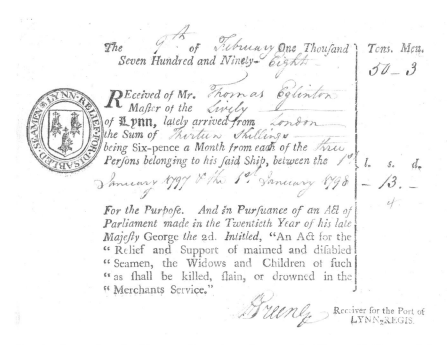

Receipt for paying the Sixpence Duty issued to captain Thomas Eglinton of the Lively *at King's Lynn in 1798.*

lost, but fortunately the records for the busiest waterway in the UK – the Thames – have survived. Ships from all around the UK docked here, not just those originally from London. As noted above, there are also some surviving records from Exeter.

An example entry from the Thames for 1728 is given below:

Where last paid	*Sandwich*
Time when paid the 6d per month	*6th March 1728*
Ship or vessel's name	*Vine*
Of what place	*Ramsgate*
Of what burthen [tonnage]	*80*
Number of men usually sailed with	6
Master's name	*William Moverly*
Whence arrived	*Seville*
To what time last paid	*30th October*
Time of the first man's entry	*11th November*
Time of the last man's discharge, or end of the voyage	*26th February*
No. of months for a man	*20*
Money received	*£0. s10. d0*

For much of the eighteenth century you will need to read each volume of accounts, one page at a time, to find an ancestor. It is quicker to scan the 'Of what place' column, if you know the port a captain operated from.

The only UK-wide record of the Sixpence Duty is for the year 1834, and it is arranged in roughly alphabetical order of port name (ADM68/218). Although incomplete, it is sometimes valuable for tracing captains in the year immediately before the introduction of merchant seamen registration (see Chapter 4).

There are three separate UK-wide registers of payment of the Seamen's Fund between 1831 and 1852 in BT167/41–53. They are arranged by date and all record the name of the captain and his ship, and may include tonnage and home port. These might be worth searching if you cannot find a captain from this period in other sources such as *Lloyd's Register*, ship registration documents, or seamen's registration schemes, but are not recommended otherwise.

Paradoxically, despite the assiduousness with which the Sixpence Duty was collected from merchant ships to support Greenwich Hospital, it was decided in Queen Anne's reign to bar merchant seamen from using it! The demands made on the hospital by the Royal Navy meant there was no room for merchant seamen. Subsequently, in 1747, shipowners and merchants petitioned Parliament for the sixpences paid by their seamen to be used to establish separate merchant seamen's hospitals, but this idea was rebuffed. Yet the merchant service was forced to continue paying the duty. This injustice was deeply resented and captains dodged payments if they could; it partly explains why some crews amassed quite substantial arrears of payments.

Mediterranean Passes
- Coverage: 1662–1850.
- Access: ADM7/75–162 and 630 at TNA.
- Information provided includes: name of captain, ship, ship type, where built, tonnage, home port, where pass granted, foreign destination, crew numbers.

It seems remarkable, but even in the nineteenth century Britain paid the Barbary pirates to stop them attacking its merchant shipping. The pirates, or 'corsairs', were based in North Africa – principally Algiers, Tunis, and Tripoli – and attacked merchant shipping for their cargoes and to take away crews and passengers as slaves. Although they operated principally in the Mediterranean, they were also active in the Atlantic. In order for their paid immunity to be recognised, British merchant ships applied for a Mediterranean Pass from the Admiralty which they could present to secure protection if accosted by a pirate. The pass could last for up to three years, after which time it had to be surrendered.

The registers of these passes still exist and date from 1662 to 1850. Note that passes were issued to ships operating anywhere in the Atlantic and Mediterranean, not just those venturing near the north African coast. There are three separate series of registers at TNA probably reflecting different places of issue. You may need to look in more than one series, depending on the era you are interested in:

- 1815–50, Mediterranean passes. ADM7/154–162
- 1729–1827, Foreign passes. ADM7/134–153
- 1662–1843, Passes. ADM7/630 and ADM7/75–133

There are indexes to registers by ship name within the 'Passes' and 'Foreign passes' series above. The index volumes tend to alternate with the registers themselves, although some are now missing. For example, ADM7/114 is the register of passes for 1795–8, and ADM7/115 is the index to ships for the same years. It is possible to look through the registers to find a named captain even if you do not know the name of his ship, but this is time consuming.

The three different series of registers contain similar information. Here is an example entry from the register of passes for 1767–9 (ADM7/94):

No. of pass	*403*
Date of certificate [i.e. date application approved]	*September 29th 1767*
Nature [ship type]	*Snow*
Ship's name	*Triton*
Of what place [home port]	*Lancaster*
Burthen [tonnage]	*70*
Guns	*2*
At what place [pass awarded]	*Lancaster*
Master's name	*John Goad*
Men	*14 British, nil foreign*
Built	*British*
Whither bound directly from the place the pass is issued at	*Jamaica*
Date of the pass	*5th October 1767*
When [the pass] returned	*21st November 1768*

You will find that some of the registers are sadly incomplete, with many empty columns, but the name of the captain and his ship is always present. From time to time, the government became aware that large numbers of their passes were being used illegally. So in some years, all passes were revoked, then re-issued. This happened in 1722, 1729, 1750, 1765, 1776, 1783, and 1802.

National Certification and Registration

A national index of ships' masters was compiled centrally between 1845 and 1854 and is kept at TNA as series BT115. It yields basic information such as age, place of birth, and voyage details. However, if you have located your ancestor in the BT113 Register of Seamen's Tickets (Chapter 4), then BT115 will not provide additional information as both are derived from the same source (crew lists). Both BT113

Inside a captain's cabin from the 1870s.

and BT115 are accessible to subscribers of www.findmypast.co.uk which is the fastest and easiest mode of access.

From 1845 onwards, a voluntary certification system was introduced for masters and mates as a means of proving they had the necessary skills and experience for command. The resulting certificates awarded, 1845–9, are in TNA series BT143, and details recorded include place and year of birth, plus current ship served on. These voluntary certifications were also posted in an appendix to *Lloyd's Register* between 1846 and 1852.

In 1850 certification became compulsory for masters and mates on foreign-going ships, and in 1854 this was extended to ships operating in home waters. It was immediately recognised as unreasonable for officers who had been doing the job for years to sit an examination, so those of long-standing were certificated based on their experience instead. Thus, two types of certificate came into being: certificates of competency (CC) required an examination; certificates of service (CS) required written proof that an officer already had sufficient seagoing experience.

A series of registers kept track of the certification process. They document the officer's place and year of birth, place and date of certification, certificate number, and coded details of voyages (TNA has a guide to voyage codes). At TNA the registers are arranged as follows, with entries ordered by certificate number:

- BT122 (1845–1906), CC, foreign trade (certificate numbers 1–34,999; 81,000–99,999; 0501–045,000)
- BT123 (1881–1921), CC, foreign trade steamships (certificates 001–0021,000)
- BT124 (1850–1922), CS, foreign trade (certificates 35,000–80,999)
- BT125 (1854–1921), CC, home trade (certificates 100,000–119,000)
- BT126 (1854–88), CS, home trade (certificates 120,000–150,000)
- BT128 (1833–1934), CC, colonial ships (all certificate numbers ending in letters).

Fortunately, one source acts as an index to all the above – BT127 is arranged alphabetically by surname and yields the certificate number, which you then use to find the detailed entries in BT122–128. The certificate number shows you which of the above registers to look in: do not ignore any zero or double zero at the beginning of the certificate number as these denote a different numbered series to those without initial zeros. The BT127 entry often gives date and place of birth, so this helps distinguish men with similar names. BT127 stops at the year 1894.

The BT122–128 registers and BT127 were replaced by a series of index cards arranged alphabetically by surname, and covering 1910 to 1969. These have been copied onto microfiche and can be found at TNA as series BT352. Each index card reveals place and date of birth, certificate number, date and place of passing examinations, date and circumstances of death if on active service, and any notable career events such as awards, extra qualifications, or disciplinary measures. They can yield valuable personal information. Thomas Scott from South Shields, for example, died of tuberculosis whilst second mate on the *Wandle* in 1943. When captain of the *Leyton*, William Brown of Devonport was fined £16 for 'proceeding to sea without a duly certificated cook' in 1925.

Note that some men who were granted a master's certificate never actually captained a ship or only did so intermittently. So, although an ancestor may be described as a 'master mariner' by virtue of being certificated, he may never have been a captain. Even when a man did become captain, this was not necessarily permanent: in circumstances where suitable work was hard to come by, a certified master would often act as a mate. This might happen when, for example, a captain's regular ship was suddenly taken in for repairs, leaving him unemployed, or because the man in question accepted a lower rank to gain experience of a new voyage route or a new type of ship.

Lloyd's Captains' Register

Lloyd's Captains' Register was instituted to record the careers of men who received a master's certificate between 1869 and 1947. It is vital to appreciate that it documents commands of foreign-going ships

Captain William Harrison of the Great Eastern *in 1859.*

almost exclusively. For example, it is generally not worth looking in this source for captains of coasters and ferries.

The original volumes of *Lloyd's Captains' Register* are kept at London Metropolitan Archives as series Ms 18567–18571, but there are microform copies elsewhere, including the Caird Library at the NMM, TNA (incomplete), and the Society of Genealogists. These copies can be hard to read – especially for early years – so you may need to view the originals.

The first run of the register is Ms 18567. It is in 87 volumes, was begun in 1869, and concluded in 1911. For captains active in 1869 their service as far back as original certification is often recorded, which in practice means that some records date back to 1851. The register shows a captain's place and date of birth, certificate number (with date and place of issue), the official number of each ship served on with dates of service and destinations, and any special extra qualifications. The voyage details generally relate to large commercial foreign-bound ships, rather than home trade, and mates are not included unless they have a master's certificate. The registers can also include details of disciplinary action or awards, as well as any serious incident at sea such as losses, collisions, and investigations, often with a reference to *Lloyd's List* (often simply quoted as a date). These details are usually recorded in blue ink. There are short printed career summaries for some captains who were active before 1869: they were cut out of a book describing captains' careers and glued into the register. This book was effectively a one-off printing of the captains' register for 1869, and London Metropolitan Archives has a copy.

Individuals are generally listed alphabetically by surname, but many are out of sequence for various reasons, which can make it easy to miss entries. Helpfully, volunteers at the Guildhall Library have indexed the majority of them for 1851–1911 at www.history. ac.uk/gh/capintro.htm. You will see an alphabetical index by surname at the foot of this webpage, but note that a few letters of the alphabet have not yet been tackled. The Guildhall's index provides the captain's name, date and place of birth, his certificate number (with city it was awarded in and year of award), and then lists volumes of the original registers to consult for details of voyages. An example entry is:

FRYER, Richard William b. Arlingham, Gloucester 1855 C030492 Bristol 1896 F&A vol. 62 1896–1900; vol. 77 1908.

To understand this, you must be aware that the Guildhall index and the registers themselves use various abbreviations to indicate the nature of a master's qualification, the type of vessel captains were certificated to command (sail or steam), and where they could sail (home or foreign waters):

- C – certificate of competency
- S – certificate of service
- CHT – certificate of competency for home trade ships only
- SHT – certificate of service for home trade ships only
- F&A – fore-and-aft-rigged ships only (i.e. sailing vessels)
- Stm – steam vessels

If a certificate was granted outside the UK it is prefixed with 'Col' (Colonial) or an abbreviation for the country concerned, e.g. 'NZ' (New Zealand).

Depending on the era, the registers adopted different methods of distinguishing captains from mates:

- Before 1869: ship's name in italics = mate; ordinary typeface = captain
- 1869–93: ship's name underlined = mate; not underlined = captain
- 1894–1911: red ink = mate; red ink and underlined = second or third mate; black ink = captain

Note that before 1893, red ink was used to show dates of discharge.

There is no online index to captains after 1911, but from 1912 to 1947 the format of the registers changed and they are arranged alphabetically by surname. Slightly confusingly, there are two registers that cover this period, known as Ms 18568 and Ms 18569. They include certificated masters but only if they were active as ship's captains from 1912 to 1947. You need to look in *both* registers to find an individual. The registers are typewritten from 1912 and so are easier to read. Each page also incorporates a guide to the abbreviations and text colours used. The dates given next to each ship's name are the date of appointment. The register may include copies of entries from *Lloyd's List* for casualties, or a note about the fate of a ship. It will sometimes record service in the RNR (see Chapter 7). Otherwise, the information contained is similar to that in the earlier versions of the register. Note that, particularly during the period of the two world wars, there may be occasional gaps in service caused by information about an officer's career not reaching Lloyd's.

Finally, Ms 18570 is a card index of master's certificate holders who only undertook the role of mate after 1912, and Ms 18571 is an index of those awarded master's certificates between 1932 and 1947 who were never appointed as master or mate during this time.

Copies of Certificates

One of the most valuable sources of information is the copy of a master's or mate's certificate with its associated paperwork. If issued before 1927, you can obtain them by visiting the Caird Library at the NMM, or you can order copies to be sent in the post for a fee (contact manuscripts@nmm.ac.uk or phone 020 8312 6516). Note that you must have the certificate number to do this. You can get a certificate number from:

- The online Guildhall index to *Lloyd's Captains' Register*
- The *Mercantile Navy List* (see Chapter 3) for certificates of competency issued between 1845 and 1864
- From BT127 (1845–94) or BT 352 (1910–69) at TNA
- Crew lists (see Chapter 4, and below)

Note that some records have not survived, or are incomplete or damaged. The certificate itself tells you the name of the officer and the date and place of his being certificated. Of more interest is the application form that had to be completed because it records each candidate's entire seagoing career to date: every ship served in with its port of registration, the man's rank, and dates of employment. The application form also shows his date and place of birth and address. Sometimes you will find correspondence accompanying these papers that can yield additional personal information.

Other Sources of Information

Crew Lists

The Crew List Index Project (CLIP) is attempting to index surviving British crew lists kept around the world from 1861 to 1913. The home page, www.crewlist.org.uk, includes a link to CLIP Finding Aids – click on this, and then choose 'Masters'. Entering your captain's surname in the search box then produces a list of named

A master's certificate of competence for Donald Bain Macintosh, issued in 1865.

captains, with their addresses, ship's name, and year. The record office holding the original crew list is also given and, as explained in Chapter 4, they usually identify each crewmember's previous ship. For more information about crew lists, the many other indexes available, and how to access them, see Chapter 4.

Welsh Officers
Around 25,000 officers operating in Welsh merchant ships from 1800 to 1945 are identified at www.welshmariners.org.uk.

Disciplinary Measures
The Registrar General of Shipping and Seamen kept so-called 'Black Books' of officers who had committed offences that warranted disciplinary action. These included negligence, drunkenness on duty, violence, and embezzlement. They also included serious crimes committed outside an officer's workplace (e.g. rape). If found guilty,

the offender's certificate was revoked temporarily or permanently, and certificate registers note this as 'BB'. The Black Books cover 1851 to 1893 and are series BT167/33–36 at TNA. They contain many cuttings from regional and national newspapers reporting allegations, investigations, and punishments. Volume BT167/37 is an index by officer's surname.

For example, George Wright, master of the *Endeavour* of Goole, was ordered to surrender his certificate in 1855 for being an habitual drunkard. Having apparently reformed, his certificate was returned to him and he became master of the *Stanley*. Yet in 1857 he was investigated again for having 'unlawfully beaten and thereby endangered the life of James Day, his apprentice, of which charge he was found guilty and sentenced to 18 months imprisonment with hard labour'. This time his master's certificate was permanently cancelled.

Pilotage Exemption Records

From 1850 onwards, suitably experienced ship's masters could claim exemption from the need to take a pilot on board when navigating certain waters. A register was kept by Trinity House until 1957 and provides age, physical description, employer, and ship's name. These records are held by the London Metropolitan Archives (CLC/526/Ms30182).

Changes of Master

For the period 1893 to 1948, TNA has registers of changes of master for British-registered ships. This series is BT336 and is arranged by the vessel's official number. Entries state the ship's name, the port where the new master embarked, the date, and the master's name and certificate number.

Newspapers and Trade Directories

Any mention of a ship in a national or local newspaper frequently cites the captain, and these can include reports of dramatic maritime incidents and adverts for sailings. Ship's masters were notable members of their communities and so newspaper obituaries are common. Trade directories may list regular local sailings and include the captain's name.

Mercantile Navy List

For the years 1857 to 1864, this publication included brief obituaries for many mates and captains (see Chapter 3). For the same time period it described awards for meritorious or heroic conduct at sea, as did the Board of Trade's *Wrecks and Casualties Returns* for 1856–76 (see Chapter 6).

Customs and Excise Records

Series CUST50–105 at TNA contains customs and excise records arranged by outport. They may mention ships and their captains but the information is hard to find as records are extensive and each volume's index can be rather general (e.g. 'smuggling') rather than naming individuals. They're worth a browse if all else fails as they date from the seventeenth century to the twentieth.

Rescue of the Distressed

TNA series ADM30/22–25 records remuneration to captains giving passage home to shipwrecked mariners or 'distressed British subjects' between 1729 and 1826. The master and the ship is named but not the rescued Britons.

I Still Can't Find Him . . .

Some suggestions, in case you cannot find a merchant service captain or mate despite a methodical search:

- Census returns do have major limitations (see Chapter 4), but don't overlook them.
- The records of retirement homes, charities, and pensions described in Chapter 2 may help you; they are mostly kept by local record offices.
- Some local archives or family history societies keep indexes of ships that operated in their vicinity, and of their captains.
- Tombstones often identify a man as a master mariner as it was a prestigious role, so explore local and national indexes to burials and memorials.
- It was common for someone to own a ship and not be its captain. The *Mercantile Navy List*, ship registration documents, and *Lloyd's Register* are very useful in this situation as they identify owners (see Chapter 3).
- If your ancestor was known as 'captain', perhaps he served in the navy, the marines, or the army. Note that the Royal Navy has used terms such as 'sailing master' (usually abbreviated to

simply 'master') and 'master's mate' and these might be confused with titles used by merchant service officers.

- A few generations of storytelling may exaggerate a seaman's role. Maybe he served in the merchant service but did not rise to officer rank. There are also many other seagoing roles such as fisherman, lifeboatman, or coastguard, and you could explore these.

Despite the importance of recordkeeping, some officers were not recorded or their details were incorrect. Even when correctly documented, certain individuals' papers are now lost or damaged. Undoubtedly, some officers dodged officialdom and never became certificated.

Engineers

Engineers became increasingly important as technology led the merchant service away from reliance on the wind to power its ships. It also became clear that the engineer's role carried a great deal of responsibility for the welfare of the ship, its cargo, and the people on board. Accordingly, a national system for certificating and registering engineers as expert officers was instituted in 1861. It was based on the model already established for masters and mates, so there were certificates of service based on experience in-post (CS), and certificates of competency assessed by examination (CC). The registers at TNA list successful applicants in numerical order of certificate number:

- BT139 (1861–1921),CC (certificate numbers 6,000 onwards)
- BT140 (1870–1921), CC, colonial (all certificate numbers ending in letters)
- BT142 (1862-1921), CS (certificate numbers below 6,000)

These registers are indexed alphabetically by surname in BT141, but some early engineers are listed in BT127 (the index of masters and mates) instead. From 1910 onwards, engineers were incorporated into the alphabetical register of merchant service officers, BT352, described above.

Engineers' certificates can be seen or ordered from the NMM if the certificate number is known, in the same way as for captains and mates (see above). Only those from 1862 to 1921 are available.

105

Second Engineer Frederick Harrison in 1902.

Officer Trainees

There were training schools for officers, and Chapter 4 provides more detail on this aspect. Many officers, but not all, were trained via apprenticeship, where they are often known as cadets. Before the mid-nineteenth century, most officers rose through the ranks from the role of seaman, and the core knowledge of all aspects of seamanship that they thus acquired was expected by their crews. However, in the Victorian era some prospective officers were appointed directly to ships as midshipmen – these were usually 'young gentlemen', the sons of relatively wealthy parents. They were trained on the job, and often had to pay for the privilege, at least at the beginning of their careers.

Telegraphers and Radio Officers

Also known as 'Marconi men' if they were employed by the Marconi company, these personnel operated the Morse code apparatus on board ships. They often later became wireless and radio operators as technology advanced. Some colleges specialised in training them (e.g. the Wireless College in Colwyn Bay, Wales), and you may be able to investigate whether local records related to these institutions

Radio Officer William Walters in 1945; his medal ribbon is the 1939–45 Star.

107

have survived. In the first few decades of the twentieth century, many telegraphers were the employees of a telegraphy company, rather than of a merchant shipping concern. The major holder of UK archives related to telegraphy companies and their activities is the Porthcurno Telegraph Museum in Cornwall, at www.porthcurno .org.uk. Contact the archives department for more information about the records it holds and whether these might assist you. The records that mention personnel mainly relate to cableships.

The Marconi Archives are held by the Bodleian Library in Oxford and include company records related to the Marconi International Marine Communication Company Limited, as well as some Marconi staff training records for the twentieth century, at www. bodleian.ox.ac.uk.

Finally, a sizeable proportion of telegraphers and radio operators were trained by the armed forces, so you could consider exploring military service records – especially for the Royal Navy – even if your ancestor was employed principally in a civilian capacity.

Cooks

Cooks were registered with certificates of competency or service from 1906. TNA holds an alphabetical register of successful applicants for 1913–56 as series BT319. The index gives name, place and year of birth, and certificate number. The original certificates have not survived, but registers of cooks are held by the NMM. You will need the certificate number from BT319 to locate an individual, but the registers rarely reveal anything more than is recorded in BT319.

Many cooks were trained at the London School of Nautical Cookery, which opened in 1893 expressly to train cooks for the merchant navy. It was housed in the Sailors' Home in Well Street (now Ensign Street), London. Although no admissions or training registers survive, there is copious correspondence and committee minutes kept as part of series SAH at the Caird Library, NMM.

Chapter 6

DISASTER AND BRAVERY

The tale of a shipwreck can provoke a wide range of reactions – fear, excitement, sorrow, outrage, curiosity, even romance. There can be a fascination to find out more – none more so than if an ancestor was involved. Yet the statistics on losses are often alarming. For example, between 1852 and 1856, a period without international conflict, a staggering 4,341 UK ships were wrecked on the British coast and there were a further 787 serious collisions. These incidents cost the lives of 4,148 people.

Even in the twentieth century, 222 oceangoing passenger ships were lost worldwide, not including those lost in the two world wars. These peacetime losses proved fatal to over 12,000 passengers and crew; seventy of the ships were British.

In this chapter I will start by explaining the various causes of a ship's demise, then introduce the resources available for researching the fate of individual vessels, and of crewmembers who died at sea. Finally, the sea can inspire astonishingly heroic behaviour and I will highlight sources where seamen's awards are recorded.

Technical Terms

There are a number of semi-technical terms used to describe a ship's ruin. Ship losses arise when a vessel sinks, disappears, or suffers enough damage for it not to be repaired. I have generally preferred the word 'loss' to the word 'wreck' because the latter can only really be used when the physical location of the ship's remains are known. Besides, the evocative word 'wreck' conjures up scenes of rigging and timber piled on the rocks, half-drowned sailors crawling ashore through the stormy waves, Grace Darling, and maybe desert islands. 'Loss' is a more neutral term.

A ship is grounded if it sticks to the sea bottom temporarily but is quickly refloated, perhaps when the tide rises. Infamously, the

Queen Elizabeth 2: *Southampton residents say the* QE2 *ran aground on its last voyage because it did not want to leave its home port.*

QE2 grounded in the Solent for forty minutes or so on its last voyage in 2008.

Stranding is a more significant problem, where a ship runs ashore or onto a sandbank and cannot be quickly refloated. If there are no rocks the vessel may be comparatively undamaged and may put to sea again. Sometimes a badly damaged ship is deliberately stranded to save it from sinking. Stranding is not the immediate cause of a vessel's loss, but it may be a precursor: in this situation a ship is more vulnerable to pounding from the sea, or storm damage.

A ship that takes on enough water to sink is said to have foundered. This can happen for many reasons, some of which are explored in the next section. A vessel that capsizes, on the other hand, remains afloat, but has turned upside down so that the hull is uppermost. Capsizing is often a forerunner to foundering. Ships are abandoned when the crew considers it too dangerous to remain on board.

Ships may be sunk deliberately and this is called scuttling. There are other methods of rendering a vessel unsuitable for future

110

seagoing service, including hulking, whereby a ship is reduced to its hull. This was commonly done to ex-navy ships in the days of sail: the masts and rigging were removed and the resultant hull and decks ('hulks') were used as floating prisons or hospitals, among other things. A ship is scrapped or broken up when it is heavily damaged, too uneconomical to repair, or out of date – the vessel is dismantled, but some of the components are often saved for later construction projects.

Reasons for Losses at Sea

There are many causes, and in practice an individual ship is usually lost because a variety of factors have acted in concert. However, the basic reasons can be grouped into a number of convenient categories.

Forces of Nature

The weather is the single biggest cause of ship losses and is almost certainly the reason for the majority of unexplained missing ships: in most cases they probably succumbed to storms. There are innumerable examples of ships being lost in this way. The worst single example is the Great Storm of 1703 which wrecked hundreds of ships, including thirteen navy vessels. The busy river Thames was strewn with wreckage the next day, and chronicler Daniel Defoe describes how all the ships on the busiest waterway in the kingdom had been blown away: 'No anchors or landfast, no cables or moorings would hold them, the chains which lay across the river for the moorings of ships, all gave way.'

The *Halsewell* is an example of a ship wrecked by a storm that is particularly notable because of the tragic and prolonged agonies of its passengers and crew, which drew much media attention at the time. Even the King requested to visit the wrecksite. In 1786, the *Halsewell* struck steep cliffs on the Dorset coast. Some of the men clambered into a cavern, in which many would later die overnight, but the captain would not abandon ship because he knew his daughters would never survive the attempt. Their cries of terror could be heard by the men clinging to the rocks. The next day, local people managed to haul survivors up the cliff face, and remarkably around eighty survived, although 160 perished.

The largest British merchant ship ever lost at sea sank during a storm. The MV *Derbyshire* went down with all hands near Japan during Typhoon Orchid in 1980. She was a combination carrier of 91,655 gross tonnage.

Yet there are meteorological phenomena other than storms that can threaten ships. Fog is a persistent offender. The RMS *Empress* was hit by a Norwegian collier in dense fog on the St Lawrence River in 1914. It foundered with alarming speed, taking over 1,000 lives with it. Although both captains blamed each other, it is clear that the fog prevented either crew recognising the other ship and their respective directions of travel until it was too late.

A number of ships have been trapped and then crushed in ice – particularly in the Baltic, north Canada, and polar regions. Perhaps most famously, Shackleton's barquentine *Endurance* was trapped in the Antarctic ice in 1915 and slowly squeezed apart until it sank. Occasionally ships are struck by lightning – the brand-new clipper ship *Golden Light* was hit by a lightning bolt, caught fire and sank off the coast of America in 1853.

Other natural forces have, very rarely, played a part in causing a ship's demise. For example, Captain Evan Jones from Portmadoc watched in dismay as a large whale rammed his schooner *Waterloo* in 1855. The ship heeled over, timbers cracking. The crew abandoned ship and looked on from the long-boat as the schooner rapidly sank beneath the waves.

Human Error

This is commonly a causative factor in the loss of ships but is sometimes the principal cause. HMS *Racehorse* was lost in 1822 when its pilot made a navigational error that resulted in the ship smashing into rocks off the Isle of Man. This event famously inspired William Hillary to establish the Royal National Lifeboat Institution (RNLI).

Before the early nineteenth century the inadequacy of sea charts was a major problem; captains needed their wits about them in certain waters. As many as 2,000 ships have been lost on the Goodwin Sands since the thirteenth century – in some cases at least partly because the sands change their position regularly, so an out-of-date chart is dangerous.

Collisions are a common cause of loss. Famously, RMS *Titanic* collided with an iceberg on its maiden voyage in 1912, but ships are much more likely to sustain damage by colliding with each other,

Drunkenness may have been a factor in the Glenesslin *running ashore and being lost.*

harbours, bridges, and other constructions. In 1799, the *Norfolk* hit Ramsgate pier with such force that its bows were stove in and it sank almost immediately. In 1873, the passenger ship *Northfleet* was at anchor off Dungeness at night and was accidentally rammed by a steamer, the *Murillo*, travelling at full speed. The *Northfleet* foundered so quickly that 320 passengers drowned, despite there being many ships nearby that could have offered assistance.

In some cases errors have been caused by drunkenness, as was alleged after the loss of King Henry I's son on board the *White Ship* in 1120. Other officers have been at fault for not posting a look-out: Captain Brooke of the *Tryall* was thus accused after running his ship onto rocks in Australia's earliest shipwreck in 1622. Most notoriously in recent times, the *Herald of Free Enterprise* sank in 1987 because the crew left the bow doors open, allowing the sea simply to rush in and swamp the ship.

Violence

Human violence is a significant cause of ship losses, particularly during wartime. However, before 1815, vessels were often captured, repaired, and brought into the service of the captor nation – sometimes retaining the same name.

The sinking of the *Lusitania* in the First World War is the most famous deliberate sinking of a merchant ship by violent means. It was carrying passengers across the Atlantic and, not engaged in warlike activities, was unarmed and without convoy, yet was torpedoed by a German submarine on 7 May 1915. This atrocity took the lives of 1,200 men, women, and children (including 128 Americans) and helped bring the USA into the war. The *Carpathia* – which ironically had rescued the survivors of the *Titanic* – was also sunk by enemy action just before the war ended in 1918.

Lusitania *was sunk by a U-boat in 1915.*

Piracy has claimed many ships. Henry Morgan sank the merchant ship *Magdalena* in 1669, for example; similarly the *Saladdin* was lost in 1844 to pirates who murdered the officers and ran the ship ashore to steal its cargo.

Fires

Ironically, although surrounded by water, ships are susceptible to fires. In the age of sail, fires were greatly feared: the dry timbers, great sails, and tar-soaked rigging were all highly flammable. Once fire took hold it was impossible to put out and incineration was inevitable. Yet tobacco smoking on board was widespread – in the navy even encouraged – naked-flame lanterns were used, and a galley fire was kept for cooking. It is a wonder more wooden ships didn't burn.

This fate befell a British East Indiaman called the *Kent* in 1825. An officer dropped his lighted oil lantern in the hold while trying to secure a cask of spirits that had broken loose. The cask split and the spirits caught alight. The fire rapidly got out of control; the ship blazed for hours before blowing up. Fortunately, most of the 640 people on board were saved, but eighty-one perished. In 1852, a similar fate befell the *Amazon,* which raced fullsteam ahead in a gale while ablaze, because the flames prevented anyone reaching the engine room to turn the ship about.

Fire has proved fatal to many ships in more recent times as well, including steel vessels. The passenger ship *Volturno*, for example, caught fire and exploded in 1913 and the cruise ship *Scandinavian Star* became a loss after an arsonist set it alight in 1990.

Instability

Construction errors, a weakened structure due to poor maintenance, and mechanical failure have led to the demise of many ships. The steamship *Lexington* caught fire and foundered in 1840. The primary reason was a design fault: the wood-burning boilers had not been properly converted to burn coal, which combusts at a much higher temperature, and consequently the engines set the ship's funnel alight. All but four of the people on board died.

Instability of cargo or its breaking free after storage often plays a part in vessels capsizing. The *Vestris* was a liner *en route* to Barbados in 1928. In a heavy sea, the cargo and some of the ship's coal broke free and set up a dangerous list which caused it to capsize part-way through its evacuation. Half of the passengers perished.

Shipowners' zeal to maximise cargo-carrying capacity sometimes yielded disastrous results. For example, in 1866 the passenger ship SS *London* was overloaded with iron and coal, and when it met violent seas, the coal broke loose and prevented the water draining away. The swamping seas put out the engine fires, and then the massive dead weight of the iron cargo put the ship at the mercy of the storm. Its disastrous loss shocked the public: only nineteen of the 263 passengers and crew were saved.

Intentional Loss

This includes scuttling, hulking, and scrapping – all of which have already been described. In 1718, the pirate Blackbeard intentionally

Captain and leading officers of SS London, *who were lost with the ship in 1866.*

116

ran aground his flagship, *Queen Anne's Revenge*, to break up his company so that they might disperse with their share of many years of ill-gotten gains.

In wartime a ship may be scuttled to stop it falling into the hands of the enemy. Similarly, captured enemy ships were scuttled if there were insufficient British crewmen to take her to a safe port. Ships are also sometimes deliberately scuttled to block entrances to waterways in wartime. In the era of sail, old ships were sometimes sunk to act as breakwaters; in more modern times, some ships have been scuttled to act as artificial reefs and places for divers to explore.

Although not destroyed, some ships have their seafaring days ended for good by serving a totally different purpose such as floating hotels (e.g. *QE2*) or museum exhibits (e.g. *Cutty Sark*).

Tracing a Lost Ship

Maybe one of your forebears was on board a vessel that got into difficulties – a passenger, crewmember, the captain, or perhaps a rescuer instead? All you may know is that a ship or an individual was lost at sea, and you want to uncover the details. Alternatively, you may have lost contact with a mariner or a ship in contemporary records and are wondering what happened. Tracing their fate can be time consuming because there is no central archive where you can look. Much digging may be required.

Before the mid-nineteenth century, many ships simply 'disappeared': they just did not arrive at their destination. There was no central registration of losses, so in this situation a modern investigation can be fruitless. You should also appreciate that it is generally easier to trace a ship than a crewmember, unless he was the captain, because few records were kept before the mid-nineteenth century of deaths at sea.

Note that for ships lost in the two world wars you should consult Chapter 7.

General Shipping Sources

Some sources for tracing a ship's loss were described in Chapter 3. You should refer to that chapter for how to access these sources, but I briefly review the information they may yield about ship losses below.

117

Lloyd's Register of Shipping

So-called 'posted' editions of *Lloyd's Register* were serially updated with information from Lloyd's and during the nineteenth century this included marking vessels as 'Lost'. This is helpful because such vessels are otherwise deleted from the subsequent edition without explanation. However, many lost ships were not marked as such and, particularly for the first half of the nineteenth century, vessels could continue to be listed for years after they ceased to exist. Despite this limitation, looking through successive editions of the *Register* until a ship is no longer listed is sometimes your only early clue to the approximate year of a ship's demise.

Since the *Register* also notes the date and nature of major repairs, it can yield clues to the timing of significant damage which the ship sustained without being lost (e.g. during a storm).

Certain *Lloyd's Register* spin-off publications can help you trace lost ships, including:

- *Lloyd's Register Wreck Returns* (or *Casualty Returns*) (from 1890) describes lost or damaged vessels from *Lloyd's Register* each quarter. Incidents are classified by cause (e.g. collision). It also lists missing and scrapped ships.
- 'Lloyd's Register Wreck Books' (1940–77) were in-house hand-written records. They describe the fate of ships deleted from *Lloyd's Register*, and may add detail not available from other sources. They are only available from Lloyd's Register head-quarters www.lr.org. Phone and ask for the archivist (tel 020 7709 9166).
- *Lloyd's Missing Vessel Books* (1873–1954) list ships reported as missing, together with master's name and voyage details. This is only available from the Guildhall Library in London. It is indexed by ship's name and is helpful because other sources do not always record ships 'missing presumed lost'.

Lloyd's List

Probably the single most important source for determining the fate of ships. Its casualties section reported everything from wrecks and disappearances to relatively minor collisions.

Lloyd's Weekly Shipping Index gives casualties for each year from 1880 to 1920. This was succeeded by *Lloyd's Weekly Casualty Report*. Both were compiled from the *List* and are bound in annual volumes indexed by ship name, which may speed your search.

Similarly *Lloyd's Captains' Register* often contains references to *Lloyd's List* – a shortcut if you know the captain's name (see Chapter 5).

When looking for an incident on a known date, bear in mind the slowness of international communications in former times. It could take a long time for news to reach London. For example, it was not until 6 December 1842 that *Lloyd's List* reported from Bombay: 'The brig *Mavis*, Jones, from the west coast (with specie) was struck by lightning and instantly blew up on 31st July, near the Grand Ladrone; crew saved.' So you may need to look for details of a loss several months after it actually happened.

The Guildhall Library in London keeps *Lloyd's Loss and Casualty Books* (1837–1972) as series Ms 14932. These usually do not add significant information to that found in *Lloyd's List*, but can be easier to search first.

Mercantile Navy List

Obituaries of officers were included from 1857 to 1864 and may provide brief accounts of a ship's loss. They are sometimes the only source – e.g. 'William Riddoch: drowned in the *Elphinston*, sailed from Cardiff Nov 29th 1859, and not since heard of.' From 1875 until 1904 there was an appendix listing ships that had ceased

SS Roebuck *on rocks off Jersey in 1911.*

119

operating since the previous edition. This incorporates lost vessels, and is often the easiest way to determine the fate of smaller British ships.

Ship Registration Documents

Details of a vessel's loss are not always documented, but scribbled across the registration paper in red ink there is often a terse statement recording its demise. For example, the barque *Renown* (410 tons) from London met its end off the Australian coast where it was 'Totally wrecked on the island of Angour, the Pellew Group, 10th Feb 1870'. Captain Thomas's vessel the *Amy*, on the other hand, was trapped in 1832 when the Baltic Sea froze and it was slowly crushed. The end for other vessels is far less dramatic: the *Telegraph*, a sloop built in South Shields in 1859, was thirty years later 'dismantled and converted into a landing stage'.

Even if the circumstances of a vessel's end are not given, the date when the register closed is usually documented, indicating the latest date it could have been lost.

Specific Sources for Wrecks

Apart from the more general sources mentioned above, there are some information sources that deal specifically with lost ships.

Books and Newspapers

These are important. Individual famous wrecks have attracted whole books about the events concerned, but helpful 'indexes' to lost ships have been published as well. Notable examples include:

- C. Hocking, *Dictionary of Disasters at Sea During the Age of Steam 1824–1962* (Naval & Military Press, reprint, 1994), an encyclopedia listing alphabetically all lost British ships over 500 tons where deaths occurred in peace and war. Only brief details are given.
- Lloyd's Register published six books by Richard and Bridget Larn entitled the *Shipwreck Index of the British Isles* between 1995 and 2002. They are arranged by geographical area, and briefly describe all ships lost on Britain's coast since 1100.
- K.G. Huntress, *A Checklist of Narratives of Shipwrecks and Disasters at Sea 1586 to 1860* (Iowa State University Press, 1979), an index of contemporary accounts of ship losses.

If you know where a vessel was lost there are books describing shipwrecks on particular parts of the British coastline (e.g. I.W. Jones, *Shipwrecks of North Wales* (Landmark Publishing, 2001)), and others dedicated to whole countries (e.g. B.D. Berman, *Encyclopedia of American Shipwrecks* (Mariners Press, 1972)).

Newspapers are invaluable for lost ships if there was heavy loss of life, a remarkable rescue, or a tragic angle. They often include eyewitness accounts, and may disclose names of survivors and the dead. Illustrated papers can provide dramatic images. Many national newspapers have a considerable historic archive online (e.g. *The Times*).

Do not overlook newspapers published local to the event (including abroad), those no longer in circulation, and specialist marine publications such as the *Nautical Magazine* (from 1832). Many newspapers are not indexed, so you might have to 'hand search' editions printed around the date concerned. If you are successful, look at the next few issues afterwards in case there are updates (e.g. bodies found, salvage) or maybe an inquest. The Caird Library at the NMM has indexes to some shipping news-papers published in the second half of the nineteenth century and the early twentieth.

Websites

Many useful websites provide free information about lost ships. The most comprehensive is Wrecksite, www.wrecksite.eu, which at the time of writing had described over 112,000 wrecks world-wide and had pictures of over 20,000. This site charts the position of sunken ships, and describes the vessel (ship type, tonnage) and its history (owner, captain, wreck date).

The Pastscape site, www.pastscape.org.uk, has catalogued many wrecks around the English coast, using sources such as the books by Larn and Hocking mentioned above, *Lloyd's List*, and parlia-mentary reports. Use the search function to input a ship's name and retrieve details of what happened to the ship, as well as a full list of references.

Monuments erected after a shipwreck sometimes list those who died, and the NMM memorials database indexes over 5,000 at www.nmm.ac.uk/memorials. You can search by names of ships or individuals, but unfortunately not by year. The RNLI has created a moving memorial to its volunteer lifeboatmen who died while trying to save others at sea, and their names have been posted online, where they are listed by date and location at www.rnli .org.uk/how_to_support_us/appeals/memorial/.

The Ship's List, www.theshipslist.com, holds details of selected wrecks, and the East India Company website records the fate of many of its enormous fleet at www.eicships.info.

Finally, there are two commercial sources. Shipwrecks UK covers the British coast and uses many sources described in this chapter, but there is a charge for searching the database at www.shipwrecks.uk.com. The International Registry of Sunken Ships is a worldwide database providing information about individual wrecks free on request, but charges for more sophisticated reports, at www.shipwreckregistry.com.

Official Registers and Reports

In certain situations the loss of a ship triggered the involvement of officialdom, leading to records which may assist the family historian. Most of the sources described below were prepared for government.

- **Admiralty Wreck Registers** (1850–4). Records ships wrecked on the British coast if lives were lost. Available at Guildhall Library, London.
- **Board of Trade** *Wrecks and Casualties Returns* (1856–1918). These were published annually and list wrecked British vessels in date order. The ship is described, its cargo, the circumstances and place of wreck, and the number of lives lost. Initially the returns only described events on the British coast where lives were lost, but from 1865 all losses were included if people died, whether in home waters or not. From 1873 all British shipping losses were included even if no one died. The name of the ship's master and owner are given from 1872 onwards.

  Copies are available in the Maritime Collection at Southampton Central Library, and the Guildhall Library, London. The Caird Library at the National Maritime Museum in Greenwich holds a partial collection.
- **Reports of inquiries into wrecks** (1876 onwards). Before 1876, official inquiries conducted into the loss or damage of a ship were recorded in the Board of Trade *Wrecks and Casualties Returns* (above), but from 1876 they were published separately. Copies are held in Southampton Central Library, but

the full texts for reports published 1876 to 1951 are available online at www.plimsoll.org/WrecksAndAccidents/wreck reports. These detailed investigations include descriptions of the event, and questioning of witnesses and persons involved. If found negligent, masters could have their licences revoked or suspended.

- **Other parliamentary reports.** The House of Commons commissioned reports on ship losses in certain circumstances in the nineteenth century. The Guildhall Library keeps a list of these and we find, for example, that there is a digest of ship-wrecks on the coast of South Africa 1838–52 in Parliamentary Papers 1852, vol. 9.

- **Hydrographic Office Records** (mainly 1913 onwards). This office has recorded locations of wrecks in coastal waters worldwide since 1913, except for the USA and Australia. It also has information on certain older British wrecks. It will conduct searches about a named wreck for a fee. See www.ukho.gov.uk (look under 'Products and Services', then 'Services'). Hydrographic offices in other countries might assist you if seeking a wreck abroad; see www.iho.int.

- **Sources at The National Archives.** TNA holds few relevant records. Local investigations and reports can be found in the customs and excise outport records (series CUST), which for some ports are quite extensive and detailed. Searching TNA's Catalogue/Discovery service by port name and date and restricting to 'CUST' will show you what is available, but records are only likely to refer to wrecks on the British coast.

  Series BT369 consists of Shipping Casualty Investigation Papers (1910–88) – which informed the official wreck inquiries described above, but they may contain additional details. Letters of the Board of Trade Marine Department (series MT4, indexed per volume or via series MT5) contains some corre-spondence about individual wrecks. There may also be details of inquiries in MT9 and 15.

Deaths at Sea

Newspapers, official wreck reports, and the NMM memorials database (above) may mention crewmen who survived wrecks or who died, but many of the sources covered so far do not iden-tify personnel, except perhaps the captain. Websites such as

The memorial in Southampton to the engineering officers lost on RMS Titanic.

www.theshipslist.com have helpfully pulled together some lists of the survivors and the dead, and newspaper reports.

Historically, some parish registers noted if a person to be buried had 'drowned'. However, before the law changed in 1808, drowned seamen were sometimes buried in unconsecrated ground because their deaths were considered unnatural. If this happened there was no parish record of burial.

Civil registration of deaths began in 1837, but if someone died at sea you may not find a death certificate if there was no body. On the other hand, when a drowned body was found and identified, the death may be registered somewhere unexpected if the ship sank a long way from a seaman's home. So, you may need to keep an open mind about potential locations for registrations of death with the General Register Office (GRO).

A GRO Marine Register exists for deaths at sea on ships registered in Great Britain or Ireland from 1 July 1837, and it is indexed separately from the rest of GRO death records. Some of these data came from deaths recorded in the logs of British ships (see Chapter 4). In the GRO register, the name of the ship is identified as place of death. However, many deaths at sea in the nineteenth century were not reported to the GRO. The GRO's Marine Register has been indexed and is available on subscription websites such as www.thegenealogist.co.uk, where it is listed as 'Overseas Marine Deaths'.

The GRO compiled registers of British citizens who were born, married, or died abroad, including on board ships. There were various mechanisms by which these deaths were notified. The resulting registers are all held by TNA, and include:

- RG32, Miscellaneous Foreign Returns (1831–1969): notifications of deaths of British citizens abroad from officials overseas; often not in English.
- RG33, Foreign Registers and Returns (1627–1960): compiled from notifications via British churches, embassies, and politicians abroad.
- RG35, Miscellaneous Foreign Death Returns (1791–1921) includes foreign death certificates and death registers kept by British embassies.
- RG36, Registers and Returns of Births, Marriages and Deaths in the Protectorates, etc. of Africa and Asia (1895–1965): civil registration notices related to British citizens.

These four series have been indexed and are available online via the subscription website www.bmdregisters.co.uk.

For seamen's deaths on board ship the crew list or log (Chapter 4) should tell you what happened and may be your only source of information before the 1880s. If the vessel was lost but the crew list has not survived and previous voyages show your ancestor as a regular crewmember, then this may be your only evidence for an ancestor's death. Deaths at sea are sometimes recorded in national registration systems for merchant seamen and officers, especially in the twentieth century – see Chapters 4 and 5.

TNA's extensive collection of wills include many for seafarers – especially those registered via the Prerogative Court of Canterbury, which dates back to the fourteenth century. These are indexed and available to view via TNA's DocumentsOnline (to be replaced by their Discovery service in due course).

TNA also has various registers that recorded lives lost at sea. Deaths were not consistently reported – especially if a ship simply disappeared – despite official mechanisms to do so. You should also realise that date of death and the date it was reported may be different, so look a few months ahead if you expect to see a death and it isn't there. TNA records below give the name of the deceased, place, date, and cause of death, and identify the ship served on, but some give additional information:

- **1798–1833**, Registers of Deceased Seamen's Wages (ADM80/6-12). This records wages owing after the death of seamen travelling to the Caribbean. If wages were collected by family members, their relationship to the deceased and address is given. Sometimes contemporary correspondence is preserved. Records available on www.findmypast.co.uk.
- **1852–89**, Registers of Wages and Effects of Deceased Seamen (BT153). Indexed by name in BT154. Extra details recorded include wages outstanding and master's name. After 1866 the deceased's age and rank is given. Most records between 1881 and 1888 are missing, but gaps can often be filled by looking in the three sources below. Records available on www .findmypast.co.uk.
- **1886–90**, Monthly Lists of Deaths of Seamen (BT156). These give age and rank of the seaman, birthplace, and last known address. Records available on www.findmypast.co.uk.
- **1882–8**, Registers of Seamen's Deaths Classified by Cause (BT157). Provides rank and age of deceased, and shipowner's name. Records available on www.findmypast.co.uk.
- **1874–88**, Registers of Deaths at Sea of British Nationals (BT159). Passengers and crew who died were listed in separate volumes for England and Wales, Scotland, and Ireland. They

record age, occupation, and address of the deceased, and can be searched online via www.bmdregisters.co.uk.

- **1891–1972**, Registers and Indexes of Births, Marriages and Deaths of Passengers and Seamen at Sea (BT334). Each entry lists the seaman's age and rank, birthplace, and address. Records available on www.findmypast.co.uk.
- **1939–46 and 1964**, Inquiries into Deaths at Sea (BT341). Letters, newspaper reports, witness accounts, and other papers concerning deaths at sea or in foreign ports. Indexed by year and then ship's name.

In addition, the NMM holds the Returns of Births and Deaths at Sea for crew and passengers from 1914 to 1964 (RSS/B/1-352). There are no returns for 1920 to 1938. The series is arranged by year, then month, and within each month entries are alphabetical by ship's name. These papers identify the deceased by name, age, rank, and address, and explain the circumstances of the death and the ship served on. Note that returns for crewmembers are listed separately from passengers – be careful when requesting original documents from the NMM archive that you request the crew versions.

A rare photograph of survivors from a late Victorian shipwreck.

Local shipwrecked sailors societies or shipping company records may assist if you are trying to trace the fate of an individual or his ship. For deaths of seamen in the world wars, see Chapter 7.

Awards for Bravery

As well as losing their lives at sea, seamen often risked them. On some occasions the risks they took were so notable that they were rewarded. Between 1856 and 1876, the Board of Trade *Wrecks and Casualties Returns* (above) described awards made to merchant seamen by the British government for saving lives. For example, in 1858, Arthur Knights, second mate of the *Northfleet* from London, was awarded a telescope for rescuing the crew of the *Hebe* in stormy weather; five other crewmembers were awarded ten pounds each. After 1861, the same publication lists awards made to British subjects by foreign governments as well. So we find that in 1864 Captain William Jones of the schooner *Orestian* from Milford was awarded a gold medal and diploma from the French government for saving the crew of *L'Esperance*.

The *Mercantile Navy List* also records awards, but these are typically private honours granted to officers by grateful passengers, foreign dignitaries, or shipowners. The early editions often cite presentations from several years before. For example, in the 1852 edition, it is reported that William Gregson, when chief mate of the *Duke of Roxborough* in 1837, was presented with a silver snuff-box 'for his exertions in saving the lives of the crew and passengers of an American vessel'.

Since 1774, the Royal Humane Society (RHS) has recognised acts of bravery that helped to save life, and awarded medals in recognition. Often these acts involve the sea. Bronze medal rolls and citations for 1837 to the twenty-first century have been published online by the Life Saving Awards Research Society at www.lsars .pwp.blueyonder.co.uk. The full details for those awarded the RHS bronze, silver, and gold medals, or in receipt of a testimonial or certificate since 1774 are kept at the London Metropolitan Archives (series LMA/4517). The first recipient of the gold medal (the 'Stanhope' Medal) was Matthew Webb, later famous for being the first man to swim the Channel. In 1873, however, when he was a seaman on board the Cunard ship SS *Russia*, he dived overboard to save a crewman. The ship was going at full speed in rough seas, and although his rescue attempt was unsuccessful, Webb had to

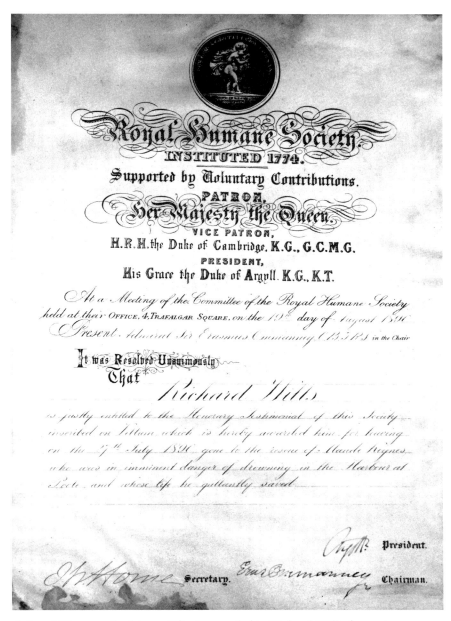

A Royal Humane Society certificate awarded to Richard Wills for saving a woman from drowning in 1890.

survive for thirty-seven minutes in the cold Atlantic before being rescued himself.

The Shipwrecked Fishermen and Mariners' Royal Benevolent Society was instituted in 1839, when it was known as the Shipwrecked Mariners' Society. It instituted the award of gold and silver medals for gallantry in 1851 and since that time has issued around six hundred. The society keeps its own records, so contact them if you wish to investigate, at www.shipwreckedmariners .org.uk.

The first state-awarded medal for heroism at sea was introduced in 1856: the Board of Trade Medal for Saving Life at Sea is better known as the Sea Gallantry Medal. A website records those who received the award from 1887 – www.searlecanada.org/hemy/ SGM001.html – and the list predominantly comprises merchant seamen, fishermen, and coastguards. Unfortunately, records for recipients before 1887 have been lost. The *London Gazette* records awards from 1926 onwards at www.london-gazette.co.uk. More details on some of the individual cases can be found in TNA series BT261.

Some shipping companies issued awards to their employees, and their records should be consulted as appropriate.

Lloyds of London issued four medals, many of which were presented to merchant seamen:

- Lloyd's Medal for Saving Life at Sea (from 1836), for rescuing or trying to rescue people in danger at sea
- Lloyd's Medal for Meritorious Service (from 1893), for preventing damage to or loss of ships and their cargoes
- Lloyd's Medal for Services to Lloyd's (from 1913)
- Lloyd's War Medal for Bravery at Sea (from 1940), see Chapter 7

The original documents describing these awards are kept at the London Metropolitan Archives (series MS 31610–31619), but medal recipients are all indexed in the book by J. Gawler, *Lloyd's Medals 1836–1989* (Howell Press, 1995).

The RNLI made awards in the form of testimonials on vellum and/or grants of money, as well as medals. These were not confined to lifeboatmen, although they do make up the majority. However, as lifeboatmen were local volunteers with seafaring experience, some of them were seamen. Details of awards and of incidents involving wrecked ships are covered in the RNLI journal *The Lifeboat* (from 1852), which is available to search in digital form in some regional archives, via certain RNLI heritage centres, or to buy (see www.rnli.org.uk). A book which describes every RNLI medal recipient, indexed by name and geographical location, is B. Cox, *Lifeboat Gallantry: The Complete Record of Royal National Lifeboat Institution Gallantry Medals and How They Were Won 1824–1996* (Spink & Son, 1998).

Certain regional bodies rewarded bravery. The Liverpool Shipwreck and Humane Society, for instance, granted both awards and medals from 1839. In 1912, it awarded medals to Captain Rostron and eight other seamen from the *Carpathia* for rescuing the *Titanic* survivors. Details of these awards are kept by the Merseyside Maritime Museum and Archives.

Quite often there was no formal mechanism to recognise heroism in a particular community, so a fund was raised locally. For example, John Blampied, master of the *Wave Queen*, was presented with a watch and silver teapot by the inhabitants of Jersey, who had raised the money by public subscription 'for his heroic conduct in rescuing twenty-two of his fellow creatures from on board the steamer *Briton* when in a sinking state during a heavy gale on the night of 11th January 1857'. In these cases the best sources for further information are local newspapers.

There are a number of national medals for gallantry which were awarded to civilians on behalf of the Crown, including the Albert Medal, British Empire Medal and George Cross (and its predecessor the Empire Gallantry Medal). The presentations of these awards were always recorded in the *London Gazette*, which you can search online at www.london-gazette.co.uk. Many of these awards, and others such as formal commendations and the OBE, were funded by the Treasury. Series T335 at TNA lists merchant navy recipients for the Second World War. Search TNA's Catalogue or Discovery Service by surname, restricting to series T335. Consult the original files at TNA for more details.

Medals awarded for military service or support are covered in Chapter 7.

Chapter 7

MERCHANT NAVY IN WARTIME

War has always posed serious threats to the merchant service. Not least, international conflict inhibits trade, which is the very reason for the existence of mercantile shipping. Vessels can be lost or damaged by the enemy, or commandeered to serve the nation's needs, and for individual seamen there is the threat of injury, death, or imprisonment. During the era of press gangs, the Royal Navy even abducted mariners and forced them to serve a military role against their will.

Yet war often presented a greater chance of promotion, allowed national recognition of meritorious conduct, and sometimes offered scope to supply new goods and services to the nation or armed forces for profit.

Warfare 1700–1815

The UK was at war almost continuously for this period, and yet trade by sea had to continue. The fate of merchant ships caught up in the conflict can sometimes be traced via *Lloyd's List* (see Chapter 6). Some ships were herded by naval escorts, or conversely chose to ignore the protection of an official convoy, so Admiralty convoy papers between 1745 and 1815 may interest you (see ADM7/60–72 at TNA), but the details they yield are rather limited. The copious Admiralty correspondence may yield further details (ADM1), as will the captain's log for the escorting warship (ADM51). A list of 180 merchant ships requisitioned by the navy between 1793 and 1803 during the wars against France and Holland can be found at ADM95/108. This records names of ships, tonnage, owners, armament, and dates of engagement, as well as the vessel's fate.

A difficult area to research is the capture of merchant seamen by the enemy. The records of seamen held prisoner abroad before 1900 are patchy, and there is no central archive. In his book *Tracing Your Naval Ancestors* (Public Record Office, 2003, pp. 122–4), Bruno Pappalardo lists TNA's holdings of imprisonment records for seamen. These mainly relate to navy personnel for the period 1779–1815, but they often include captured merchant seamen and privateer crews.

Press Gangs

More formally known as the Impress Service, Royal Navy press gangs forced civilians to serve on fighting ships against their will. Impressment had its origins in medieval times, and operated until the early nineteenth century, yet its heyday was the eighteenth century, when the navy needed a continuous supply of crewmen. Seamen working on merchant vessels were prime targets because they already had shipboard skills. Compared to the merchant service, naval recruits were badly paid, and the conditions on board ship were poorer. The navy also removed seamen from their families for years on end and many, of course, never returned.

The Impress Service was allowed to recruit able-bodied British

The press gang at work.

men with seafaring experience over eighteen years of age or under fifty-five. Essential mercantile officers such as the captain, carpenter, and mate were exempt, and men from outward-bound merchant ships were also not supposed to be pressed. In practice, all these rules – and others – were ignored when it suited the navy. Men were taken either in ports by roaming press gangs, or off merchant ships at sea by desperate naval captains who were short-handed.

The navy did not maintain an index of pressed men, but warships kept musters as a regular 'roll-call' of every man on board, and TNA holds these as series ADM36–39 for the eighteenth century, indexed by warship name and date. These musters sometimes show men forced into the navy as 'prest'. However, many pressed men were persuaded to 'volunteer' after capture to earn the bounty and advance in pay that volunteers received. In these cases there is no documentary evidence of their impressment.

Some seamen were issued with protection certificates, which they carried about their person as proof of exemption. The registers of impressment protections that have survived at TNA are:

- 1702–3 (ADM7/363)
- 1711–12 (ADM7/364)
- 1740–1828 (ADM7/365-400)

The entries identify the man's name, his occupation, the ship served on, and its tonnage. The ship's home port may be missing, but men working in one place or for the same company are often recorded together. The registers list men by date of protection being granted. They are not arranged alphabetically or geographically, nor are they indexed, so you need to search each volume, one page at a time, to find an ancestor.

Usually the master of a ship covered by a protection was identified, then the *number* of crew protected, rather than individual names, so there is a greater chance of identifying captains from these records than other ranks. For example, in 1741, Charles Birkhead, master of the East India Company's 495-ton *Queen Caroline*, was given a protection for up to forty seamen and sixty landsmen. Masters of ships were considered exempt from impressment, so many captains are not listed unless performing duties that warranted special notice (e.g. supplying goods to the military).

Impressment declined rapidly after 1815.

Privateers

In wartime, the British government could license privately owned ships to attack the enemy. These privateers captured the ships and cargoes of enemy nations, and sold them for profit, so they were something in-between maritime mercenaries and licensed pirates. A ship captured from the enemy was called a 'prize'.

From the sixteenth to the early nineteenth centuries, many merchant seamen and officers were attracted to this life, lured by the possibility of quick income. Such was the attraction that some owners did not need to pay wages – the anticipation of prize money was enough to draw a crew. Privateer ships were often pre-existing merchant ships, suitably armed, but some were purpose-built as private warships.

There are records of the activities and senior crewmembers of privateers, although little of consequence regarding non-officers.

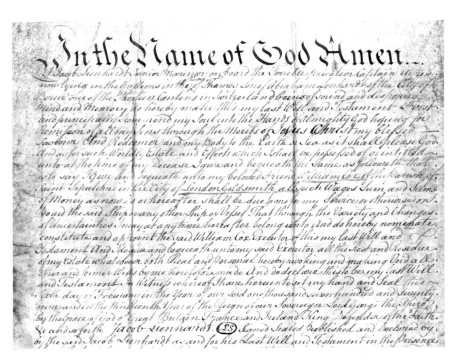

The will of mariner Jacob Lienhardt. He was dead within a year of joining Captain Ayres' London-based privateer The Terrible *in 1779.*

The online index to *Lloyd's List* (see Chapter 6) often reveals the actions of British privateers, identifies captains, and records capture of British merchant ships by enemy privateers. Various other eighteenth-century newspapers reported privateer activities, including the *London Gazette* – see www.london-gazette.co.uk. *Lloyd's Register* lists some British privateers until the 1780s.

Most records of privateers are kept at TNA. To understand them, you need to know how privateers were registered. The owners of the privateer ship were given a warrant to obtain a commission to act against the enemy, known as a letter of marque. They had to offer financial security to the Admiralty in case of any misdemeanour by the crew. This was done via a written bail (or bond). Once the bail was paid, the privateer was given a letter of marque, and the owners completed a declaration, certifying that the ship was suitably armed and crewed. TNA records consist of:

- **Privateer bails, bonds and warrants** (1549–1815, series HCA25). These are filed in date order of approval, but not indexed. They identify shipowners and the captain, and report the size, armament, and name of the ship. Other crewmen are not named. They record that financial surety is paid, and specify the nationality of ships to be attacked.
- **Privateer declarations** (1689–1809, series HCA26). These are the most comprehensive documents, and therefore the most useful. They identify the ship's master (referred to as 'commander'), and other leading crewmembers such as the second-in-command (lieutenant or mate), gunner, boatswain, carpenter, cook, and surgeon. The ship's tonnage, armament, and complement is given. Crew numbers are large because enemy ships had to be boarded, overpowered, then sailed home. The owners are identified and their place of residence. Until 1783, each volume is indexed. Declarations for certain years are reproduced on TNA's website (1689–97, 1744, 1756–61). Type an ancestor or ship's name into the Catalogue, or use the advanced search in the Discovery service, and restrict to HCA26. For privateers active against America, copies of declarations for 1812–15 (from HCA25/205–7) are available online at www.1812privateers.org (click on Great Britain).
- **Register of letters of marque**. The awards of letters of marque were written into registers which survive at TNA for 1777–1815 as series ADM7/317–332 and 649. Entries are brief,

but indicate ship name, tonnage and armament, commander, crew numbers, and the enemy nation to be attacked. There is an index to registers by ship and captain's name for privateers acting against France 1793–1815 (ADM7/328 and 649) at http://www.1812privateers.org (click on Great Britain).

- **Legal proceedings**. Before a prize could be formally handed over to privateers ('condemned'), the legal legitimacy of the enemy ship's capture was assessed by a Prize Court. These proceedings are in series HCA32 at TNA (1664–1815), and describe the captured ship, its contents, and the privateer. The List and Index Society has partly indexed HCA32 by captured vessel's name (indexes 183, 184, and 194 cover 1776 to 1817). Further information about Prize Court decisions can be found in HCA34, 46, and 48.

  Legal disputes often arose concerning privateers' activities. Many of these are described in Courts of Chancery and Exchequer papers. In TNA's Catalogue or Discovery service look under captain's surname or ship's name in series C or E.

- **Wills of privateers**. TNA's DocumentsOnline/Discovery service includes nearly 400 privateer wills at www.nationalarchives.gov.uk/documentsonline. Many originate from the Peculiar Court of Canterbury, a favoured place for seafarers to register their wills.

Warfare After 1815

There were few wars involving the sea in the Victorian era. The next major conflicts involving the merchant navy were the world wars.

Reservists and Support for the Royal Navy

The merchant service has always supplied the Royal Navy with crewmen, though not always willingly. However, once impressment was abandoned, a proper reservist force was created in 1859 that recruited merchant navy seamen and officers who were paid to undertake naval training (e.g. in gunnery). This Royal Naval Reserve (RNR) could be hastily deployed should the military need arise. By the end of the nineteenth century the RNR had over 20,000 recruits.

The RNR should be distinguished from the Royal Naval

Royal Naval Reserve seamen in 1909.

Volunteer Reserve (RNVR), which was established in 1903. The RNVR was also a reserve force, but did not employ merchant seamen so will not be discussed further here. In 1958, the RNR and RNVR were merged into a single unit now called the RNR.

RNR Officers

RNR officers were recorded in the *Navy List* from 1862. Some subscription genealogy websites have copies of certain years of this publication (e.g. www.familyrelatives.com and www.thegenealogist. co.uk) while www.navylistresearch.co.uk will hunt out *Navy List* citations for you for a fee. The *Navy List* records an officer's rank, date of appointment ('commission'), and identifies ships served on, but note that public editions printed in the world wars were edited for security reasons and so are incomplete. TNA holds the *Confidential Navy Lists* as series ADM177, which are comprehensive for wartime. The RNR is a separate section in each *Navy List,* and officers are listed alphabetically.

The creation or promotion of RNR officers is usually recorded in the *London Gazette*, even if they were temporary wartime appointments; see www.london-gazette.co.uk.

TNA holds service records for RNR officers from 1862 to 1920 (and for some honorary officers up to 1960) as series ADM240. These record service in both merchant navy and Royal Navy in order of date of commission. Depending on the era, entries may include master's certificate number, date of birth, address, ships served on, and details of next of kin. The books also include specialist officers (e.g. engineers) and the most junior officer rank of midshipman. Unfortunately, ADM240 as a whole has not been indexed, although around twenty-five of the eighty-eight volumes in the series do have some form of index by surname.

Of special interest is ADM240/84–88, available on microfilm in TNA; it indexes RNR officers active from 1914 to 1921. The index provides a volume number and page number (e.g. 5-128 means volume 5, page 128). The service records that this index refers to are in ADM240/37–50. To find out which document corresponds to the volume you require, use the TNA online Catalogue or Discovery service; in this example, volume 5 is ADM 240/41. Once you have the document number for the particular service record volume, you need to order it as an original document because this series is not available on microfilm. Service records indicate rank, ships served on, awards, medical history, comments on ability, and home address. The explicit details afforded to family historians are often fascinating. For example, Reginald Greenhough's captain noted he was a gifted artist who was also 'cool under fire', while poor Robert Gilmour's career progress was severely hampered by repeated bouts of gonorrhoea – much to the annoyance of his superiors.

Confusingly, at the same time as keeping service record books, the navy also began to maintain a card system for its officers. This is ADM340 (1880–1960 approx), which may repeat information found in ADM240, or add to it. It is worth checking both. ADM340/1–150 are service record cards for officers born before 1900 in alphabetical order and are available in full via TNA's DocumentsOnline/Discovery service. For example, William Sinker from Cambridge had been master of the schooner *Southern Cross*. He was serving with the RNR when the First World War broke out, was appointed to the temporary rank of lieutenant, and took command of the *Excellent* and *Redoubtable* to patrol harbours in south-east England.

A list of RNR officers in the Second World War is given in BT164/23, available to download from the TNA website. Unfortunately, first names are only given by initial letters and other details are scant. However, this same source also identifies officers' awards, as well as those who died, were captured, or went missing during the war.

The Unit Histories website, www.unithistories.com, describes the careers of many RNR officers from the Second World War. To find them, click on 'Officers' on the home page, then 'British Royal Navy'. There is a large database of RNR officers, providing name, rank, date of birth and death where known, decorations, and career history. Much of the information is taken from the *Navy List*, but many other sources are used, including accounts from relatives and colleagues – there are photographs of some officers.

For RNR officers who served between 1929 and 1950, service records are held by TNT Archives Services on behalf of the navy (phone 01283 227913 or email navysearch@pgrc.tnt.co.uk).

RNR Ratings

Unfortunately, most early service records for RNR ratings were destroyed. Series BT164 at TNA contains 9,000 records that have survived, all for men born before 1889 and enlisting in the RNR before 1914. These papers are indexed by surname and available in full via DocumentsOnline (due to be replaced by the Discovery service). They show date of birth, a physical description, address, parents' names, and both merchant navy and Royal Navy employment.

For RNR ratings serving between 1908 and 1955, TNA holds record series BT377/7 on microfiche. This provides similar information to BT164. For example, Roderick Garnet from 49 Cholmley Street, Hull, was the son of Mary and Daniel Garnet. He was twenty-eight when he joined the RNR in 1914, and was 5 feet 6 inches tall with fair hair, blue eyes, and tattoos of a sword and a white ensign on his arms. He served on five ships before demobilisation in 1919 and was awarded two medals.

These service documents are indexed by service number, which you can find by consulting two microfilm indexes. The index in BT377/8-27 is arranged alphabetically by surname for men serving

1908–22; the index in BT377/1–6 is alphabetical for service after 1922.

Royal Naval Division

There is another way to find out about what RNR recruits did during the First World War – both ratings and officers. The large number of reservists available when war broke out were surplus to requirements, consequently many were formed into a 'seamen's army' to fight on land with the regular army. This was known as the Royal Naval Division (RND) and was split into battalions named after famous British naval officers and ports. The service records for over 50,000 men deployed in this way are in series ADM339, available in full via DocumentsOnline (which is expected to be replaced by the Discovery service). They record date of birth, rank, career history in the RND (e.g. place of deployment, injuries, death), and name and address of next of kin. For ratings, a physical description was often given.

For example, Frederick Harwood was a stoker from Rankin Street, Liverpool, who joined the RNR and then the Anson Battalion of the RND. He was promoted to petty officer in 1915, but then was shot in the leg in the Dardanelles campaign. His medical condition was so serious that his wife, Matilda, was informed. However, after stays in various military hospitals abroad, he was invalided back to England in 1916 and survived the war pursuing shore-based duties.

Merchant Navy Reserve Pool

The lack of suitable crews could prevent ships sailing in wartime, so in 1940 the government established a national reserve pool for merchant seamen. This formed the basis of the Central Register of Seamen set up in 1941 (Chapter 4). For the first time, merchant seamen who registered with the reserve pool were paid both at sea and when they were ashore waiting for a suitable ship.

The reserve pool records are kept at the National Maritime Museum, Greenwich. They are arranged alphabetically and list date of registration with the pool, rank, date of birth, and next of kin. Very helpfully for those constructing a seaman's career, they also record the most recent ship served on. Applications for identity cards accompanying some entries may contain a photograph.

Royal Fleet Auxiliary

The Royal Fleet Auxiliary (RFA) was created in 1911 and served the navy's needs by supplying ships for transporting men, ammunition, fuel, and supplies. The crews and officers were often merchant seamen and RNR personnel, and their careers can be traced via the normal civilian or RNR routes already described. However, the RFA Historical Society maintains an invaluable website that records the careers of many personnel – both officers and ratings. Use the Search Site function on the home page at www.historicalrfa.org.

OUT FOR VICTORY.

First World War recruitment advertisement for merchant seamen.

THE MERCHANT SEAMAN.
Going home to sign on again.

Service in the World Wars

During both world wars, Britain relied on merchant ships to bring in vital raw materials, food, fuel, and to transport military equipment and personnel. Germany worked tirelessly to interrupt this lifeline, using U-boats, warships, mines, and aircraft to destroy or disable Allied merchant vessels. The Atlantic Ocean was the principal site of action because it connected the UK with its allies in North America. Hence in the Second World War this arena became known as the Battle of the Atlantic. Churchill revealed that this theatre of war had given him most concern during the conflict because of its potential to deprive Britain of essential supplies. However, vessels were also targeted on other sea routes such as the North Sea, the Mediterranean, and routes connecting Europe to Africa.

For the first time in warfare, the combatants attacked passenger ships as well as cargo vessels. The most notorious example from the First World War was the *Lusitania*, which was sunk by a German U-boat in 1915 killing around 1,200 people. In the Second World War, a passenger liner was the first merchant ship sunk by the Germans: the *Athenia* was torpedoed within a few hours of hostilities being declared.

During the First World War, the Admiralty had been reluctant to escort merchant ships at sea, believing it was ineffective and not a good use of naval resources. However, in the Second World War it escorted convoys from the start, despite a limited supply of warships. Merchant ships were often hastily fitted with light armament, but these were a minor deterrent.

For details of merchant navy personnel's service in either world war, you may be able to use seamen's registration records or crew lists (see Chapter 4). For officers, the various records described in Chapter 5 will assist you. Some merchant seamen joined the Royal Navy so may be traceable via military service records.

First World War
There were no national wartime service records for merchant seamen unless they joined the RNR or RND (see above). Crew lists are the only reliable source of information (see Chapter 4). TNA is indexing all 1915 crew lists by name for completion in 2014. Enter a surname into the Catalogue or Discovery Service and restrict to BT400.

British and Allied merchant seamen imprisoned at Brandenburg Camp in 1916.

There are records of merchant seamen who became prisoners of war at TNA as a series of lists compiled by the Ministry of Transport: MT9/1039, 1098, 1238, 1991, 5998. The longest list is MT9/1238, containing over 3,250 names and compiled in May 1918, and this has been comprehensively indexed online at http://wanborough.ukuhost.co.uk/POW/POW.htm. It records name, site of imprisonment, rank, UK address, year of birth (or age), and ship.

The records of the Foreign Office's Prisoner of War and Aliens Department is series FO383 at TNA. There are lists of merchant seamen prisoners held by enemy powers in various locations and at various times during the First World War. These include FO383/28, 35, 64, 65, 149, 202, 244, 296, 352, 382, 386, and 446. This series also has correspondence about the fates of crews of specified ships or named individuals so it is worth using the Catalogue or the advanced search function in the Discovery service to search FO383 by name.

Many merchant seamen taken by German forces were imprisoned at Ruhleben and Brandenburg Camps.

Second World War

Around 185,000 merchant seamen served their country in the Second World War, so where merchant navy records have survived they can be extensive. It is therefore important to have as much information about an ancestor as possible from family sources before hunting further, so you can narrow down your options.

The Merchant Navy Reserve Pool has already been mentioned as a source (see above), but there are other valuable records. For example, series BT390 at TNA is a series of 'pouches' recording merchant seamen's service with the Royal Navy under what were called T124X or T124T agreements for merchant seamen serving on armed ships or tugs respectively. The BT390 pouches provide information about ships served on and dates, rank, conduct, medical certificates, physical description, place and date of birth, and name and address of next of kin. You must visit TNA to see them, but they are arranged alphabetically by surname in boxes and the TNA Catalogue/Discovery service identifies which box you need. For example, BT390/140 contains records for 'Forrest H' to 'Fraser W'. BT391 is organised similarly, but covers merchant seamen who served with the navy during the Liberation of Europe (1944–5).

If your ancestor served on a merchant ship destroyed by the enemy in the Second World War, you should consult the series of Admiralty survivor's reports in series ADM199/2130–2148. These volumes are in date order, but each one is indexed by name of ship and interviewees at the front. The Admiralty interviewed survivors to gain intelligence on enemy tactics, and although not every shipping loss led to a report, the vivid firsthand accounts can reveal what actually happened to an ancestor or their ship. For example, Captain William Dowell of the SS *Empire Thunder* was in a convoy bound from Liverpool to Vancouver in January 1941. He already had four men in a boat over the starboard side inspecting his ship because of an earlier attack, and describes the moment when a German U-boat torpedo hit:

> I was on the bridge and furthest away but I saw the torpedo quite distinctly. It had a small propeller on the front and was silvered all over.
>
> It passed right through the starboard forward boat killing the four occupants outright, and struck the vessel right under

A merchant navy crew survives an Atlantic crossing in 1940.

the after bulkhead in the engine room about 250ft from the bows. There was a colossal explosion and a great amount of water and debris thrown up. One man who was standing on the boat deck was temporarily blinded by the explosion and had all his clothes blown off. I have had previous experience of being torpedoed but I have never seen so much damage done by one torpedo. The deck houses just didn't exist any more; all beams and hatch covers were blown off; it completely wrecked from no. 4 hatch, through the engine room, boiler room, no. 2 and 3 hatches and right up to the midships accommodation. The saloons were blown to pieces and the Wireless Operator told me later that all the works were blown out of the wireless room. Even the starboard davits were blown out of their sockets.

The vessel began to sink very rapidly and so I ordered the remaining crew on to a raft. I stepped off on the port side and just then saw the conning tower of a submarine about one mile distant.

TNA keeps prisoner of war records for merchant seamen captured in the Second World War. There are two separate series of records – one is arranged alphabetically by ship name (BT373/1–359), and the other by seaman's surname (BT373/360–3716). You can search TNA's Catalogue/Discovery service, by surname or ship name, and restrict to BT373.

The two series contain different information and are not cross-referenced – so you may find more information if you look at both. The 'ship' series (BT373/1–359) largely comprises letters and reports about imprisoned seamen who worked on the ship concerned, and can include details of next of kin and employer. The 'seamen' series (BT373/360–3716) describes the detention of individual seamen, and is mainly concerned with repatriation. TNA also holds an index to merchant seamen captured in the Second World War (BT373/3717) and a list of those who died in captivity (BT373/3720–3721).

As part of the fifth register of merchant seamen (Chapter 4), many records of seamen who were imprisoned or interned during the Second World War were collated centrally as a separate series within the whole. This is series BT382/3232–3251 at TNA, which is arranged alphabetically by surname. Captured RNR officers are listed in BT164/23, which can be downloaded from the TNA website.

Medals for Military Support and War Service

Pre-First World War

Military medals that merchant seamen could receive before 1914 include the 1882 Egyptian Medal (recipients recorded in TNA series ADM171/41), the 1884–5 Soudan Medal (ADM 171/42–43), and the 1899–1902 Sea Transport Medal, which was awarded for transporting troops to South Africa and China (ADM171/52).

RNR Long Service and Good Conduct Medal

This was awarded for fifteen years' service, although war service was considered 'double time'. The medal was first presented in 1909 and records of recipients up to 1950 can be found in TNA series ADM171/70–72. These digitised records can be downloaded from the TNA website at www.nationalarchives.gov.uk/documents online/digital-microfilm.asp. Similar surnames are grouped within the register, so that it is in quasi-alphabetical order (e.g. Brown, Bowen and Box are all listed together).

The World Wars

Certain wartime awards and commendations are listed in the *London Gazette* at www.london-gazette.co.uk, but the newspaper report can occur some time after the award. Do consider that in both world wars, certain merchant seamen could have received military decorations appropriate to navy personnel because of an RN or RNR role. Fifteen members of the RNR and five men serving in the RND were awarded Victoria Crosses in the world wars. TNA records for this medal are searchable online at www.national archives.gov.uk/documentsonline/victoriacross.asp.

Otherwise there were specific entitlements to medals for merchant seamen in each world war:

First World War. Medals for this war were awarded automatically to those who were entitled – seamen did not need to apply for them. Men serving in the merchant navy or RNR could be awarded the British War Medal, the 1914–15 Star, and the Victory Medal. TNA keeps records of these awards on microfilm as series ADM171, where the three medals are referred to as 'B', 'ST' and 'V'

The obverse and reverse of the Mercantile Marine Medal from the First World War.

149

respectively, and the name of the ship served on (or its official number) is also recorded. These files have been digitised and can be downloaded from the TNA website at www.nationalarchives .gov.uk/documentsonline/digital-microfilm.asp, with recipients listed in alphabetical order. It is not obvious from the download page, but RNR ratings are ADM171/120–124, RNR officers are ADM171/92–93, and merchant seamen (all ranks) are ADM171/ 130–133.

Seamen who served for six months or more during the war and entered an area where the enemy was active were awarded the Mercantile Marine Medal and the British War Medal together. They can be identified from TNA series BT351/1/1–2, which is arranged alphabetically by surname. The Silver War Badge was granted to those who became unfit for service due to an injury sustained in wartime, and 155 merchant seamen received this award, as detailed in series MT9/1404. You can search the TNA database for recipients of the Mercantile Marine Medal and Silver ward Badge via DocumentsOnline or the Discovery service. Using advanced search, restrict your search to 'WW1 Merchant Seamen Medal Cards' in the 'Categories' section.

Second World War. Seamen had to apply for their medals, so some individuals who were entitled to them may not have claimed them. At TNA there is an index to merchant seamen who received medals (series BT395) and this is available in full via Documents Online or the Discovery service. Enter a name into advanced search and confine to 'WW2 Seamen's Medals'.

The eight medals to which merchant seamen were entitled are described below, but there were more precise award criteria than this, and they were enforced strictly. The medal name is followed in parentheses by its abbreviation in BT395.

- Africa Star (AF) – for service off the coast of North Africa between June 1940 and May 1943
- Atlantic Star (AT) – for service during the Battle of the Atlantic (1939 to 1945), or on Russian convoys.
- Burma Star (BU) – for serving in the Bay of Bengal during the Burma campaign between December 1941 and September 1945.
- France and Germany Star (FR) – for supporting land oper-

Second World War medals. From left to right: 1939–45 Star, Atlantic Star (with France and Germany clasp), Burma Star, Italy Star, War Medal.

ations off the coast of France, Germany, Belgium, or the Netherlands between June 1944 and May 1945.

- Italy Star (IT) – for Mediterranean service between June 1943 and May 1945.
- Pacific Star (PA) – for serving in the Pacific or Indian Ocean between December 1941 and September 1945.
- War Medal (WM) – for those who qualified for a Star, but who died, were disabled, or captured.
- 1939–45 Star (1939) – required at least six months' service and at least one voyage into an area where the enemy might be encountered. In many cases, those seeking other medals had to earn this one first (e.g. Atlantic, Burma, Italy, and Pacific Stars).

The records specify seamen's names and discharge numbers; many also include date and place of birth. The award of a clasp (CL) indicates qualification for a second Star from a group where only one was allowed, whereas an oak leaf emblem (OLE) usually means a mention in dispatches.

The Second World War also saw the introduction of the Lloyd's War Medal for Bravery at Sea by Lloyd's of London. There were 541 recipients of this award, mostly merchant seamen, and a full list is provided at http://en.wikipedia.org/wiki/Lloyd%27s _War_Medal_for_Bravery_at_Sea.

Awards made to RNR officers in the Second World War are listed in BT164/23, available from the TNA website. These include civil honours (e.g. OBE), military awards (e.g. Distinguished Service Cross, DSC), and mentions in dispatches (MID).

Deaths at Sea

The Commonwealth War Graves Commission database at www.cwgc.org lists war dead from both conflicts including those serving with the merchant navy. The database identifies personnel who died on land and sea, and those whose bodies were never found. On the 'Search Our Records' page you can restrict your search to the merchant service by choosing it from the drop-down options under 'Force'. Each entry provides name, rank, date of death, age, and the location of a grave or commemoration.

The Commonwealth War Graves Commission website stops in 1948. The Armed Forces Memorial website begins in this year, and commemorates members of the armed forces killed on duty since then: www.veterans-uk.info/afm. The two websites operate similarly, but the Armed Forces Memorial site reports individuals' dates of birth and the ship served on. The merchant navy is not listed as a force, but RNR personnel are listed under Royal Navy.

The Merchant Navy Memorial at Tower Hill, London, commemorates over 36,000 named members of the merchant service who died in the two world wars. The Commonwealth War Graves Commission database indexes all these citations as well as personnel who were buried at various locations. Helpfully, a website records all the individual citations at Tower Hill, and lists them by ship served on: www.benjidog.co.uk.

TNA holds the Returns of Deaths of Seamen for the world wars, which record the deceased's name, age, rank, birthplace, address, and the ship served on at time of death. These documents are identified as follows:

- First World War: BT334/62 for 1914, BT334/65 (1915), BT334/67 (1916), BT334/71 (1917), BT334/73 (1918)
- Second World War: BT334/93 (1939), BT334/96 (1940), BT334/98 (1941), BT334/99 (1942), BT334/102–103 (1943), BT334/104 (1944–5).

The series BT339/3–4 is a roll of honour for merchant seamen who died in the Second World War, arranged alphabetically. BT339/6 is a similar roll for First World War merchant navy officers from 1916 to 1920 (including copies of *London Gazette* obituaries).

TNA also holds a set of Inquiries into deaths at sea (BT341) covering 1939–46 – see Chapter 6. Deaths of RNR officers in the Second World War are listed in BT164/23, available via the TNA website.

Ship Movements and Losses

Once you identify an ancestor's ship, you will want to know more about it – its role, appearance, and voyages. Wartime newspapers can help, but censorship limits their usefulness. Over 8,000 British merchant ships were destroyed in the two world wars, and if you are trying to find one the resources for lost ships described in

The Swiftsure *was lost when hit by a German mine near the Orkney Islands in 1917.*

Chapter 6 will assist you – in particular, the Wrecksite database and *Lloyd's War Losses*.

The U-boat website identifies all Allied merchant ships attacked by U-boats in either world war and gives details of the events and the crewmen lost, at http://uboat.net. Other sources specific to either conflict are described below.

If your ancestor's ship was actually sunk in the First World War, then the Naval-History.net website is valuable: www.naval-history.net/WW1LossesBrMS1914-16.htm. This lists every merchant ship lost in date order and provides name, type of ship, tonnage, location of incident, cause of loss, and the number of men who died or were captured.

Unfortunately, for much of the First World War the Admiralty did not support the concept of merchant ship convoys with navy escorts, so central accounts of merchant vessel voyages are limited. When convoys did sail, they are often described in the Admiralty war diary ADM137 at TNA, but this source can be difficult to find your way around. Similarly, the collected Ministry of Shipping papers (TNA series MT25) are quite expansive and only date from 1917, yet may provide information if you have patience. For merchant ships that were attacked by U-boats after March 1915, the series ADM131/113–117 is easier to use. If possible, consult the log for the ship you are interested in, or if that ship was lost, the log of other ships sailing with it as these often give an account of losses and rescues (see logs in Chapter 3).

There are better records for the Second World War because merchant ship movements were officially recorded and have been preserved in series BT389 at TNA. These records have been digitised and can be searched by ship's name in the DocumentsOnline section of the TNA website at www.nationalarchives.gov.uk/documentsonline/bt389.asp (although this is expected to be replaced by the Discovery service). The entries describe the ship's destination, cargos, any damage sustained in action, and its sinking if applicable. Crewmen are not identified. For example, the records for the *Laconia* show its owners (Cunard), maximum speed (16.5 knots), date of construction (1922), and details of its voyages right up to the time it was torpedoed on 12 September 1942.

Series BT347 records shipping losses day by day and includes losses due to accidents or storms as well as those occasioned by enemy action. There is an alphabetical index by ship name at BT 347/8.

Second World War convoys are identified at TNA in series ADM199/2184–2194. These Admiralty reports are in date order and describe the merchant ships involved, their escorts, cargoes, destinations, and fates. There are more detailed reports for convoys sailing between 1941 and 1945 in ADM199/2099–2102 and in ADM237, although some of these records are missing. The Convoy Web website provides detailed accounts of the sailing schedules and fates of Second World War convoys, culled from TNA Sources and beyond www.convoyweb.org.uk. Information on First World War convoys is also being accumulated for eventual inclusion.

The Battleship Cruisers website lists all merchant ships lost or damaged in the Second World War in date order at www.battle ships-cruisers.co.uk/merchant_navy_losses.htm. It records name, type of ship, tonnage, and cause of loss. A separate database accessible from this webpage records merchant vessels damaged during the conflict.

Chapter 8

PLACES TO VISIT

There are various places you can visit to extend your research into merchant navy ancestors – either to look for information about a named person or to provide an insight into their experiences.

Maritime Archives in the UK

The National Archives (TNA) at Kew holds the most important and extensive maritime documents for the UK, and has been referred to frequently throughout this book. Its Research Guides about merchant seamen give invaluable insight into the contents of TNA's collection and how to access it: www.nationalarchives .gov.uk. The National Archives of Scotland also has some maritime documents of national importance: www.nas.gov.uk.

Regional and local archives often hold important maritime documents, and two databases will help you discover who holds what:

- Access to Archives (A2A) catalogues the contents of many English and Welsh archives: www.nationalarchives.gov .uk/a2a/
- ELMAP is the University of Exeter's database of records with maritime and naval significance held in archives across England and Wales: http://centres.exeter.ac.uk/cmhs/ ELMAP/.

However, there are a number of archives with dedicated maritime collections of national importance. If you decide to visit any of these, do confirm opening times before you travel. Also check whether you need to book a seat and what form of identity to bring.

Caird Library, National Maritime Museum, Greenwich

www.nmm.ac.uk/researchers/
Unique original documents include the UK's collection of masters' certificates and application forms dating from 1850, the Marine Society's registers of merchant navy apprentices from 1772, *Lloyd's Register* surveys of merchant ships from 1834, and selected UK crew lists after 1860. There is a collection of over 250,000 maritime photographs, the world's largest collection of ship plans, and a very extensive maritime library. The website's catalogue identifies most documents in the collection.

Merseyside Maritime Museum Archives, Liverpool

www.liverpoolmuseums.org.uk/maritime/archive/
Liverpool was the second biggest port in the British Empire and so this collection is important for those with maritime ancestors, whether from Merseyside or not. There are ship registration documents dating back to 1739, information about local shipping companies and seamen's charities, and a large collection of books and photographs. The website includes an impressive collection of seventy-five information sheets describing research strategies for investigating many different aspects of the merchant navy, from women at sea to emigration.

Southampton Archives and Library

www.southampton.gov.uk (look under Archives and Library)
The Civic Centre houses the Central Library, which has a collection of maritime books, including good runs of the *Mercantile Navy List* and *Lloyd's Register*, as well as copies of Board of Trade *Wrecks and Casualties Returns* (1856–1918) and *Reports of Inquiries into Wrecks* (1876 onwards). Also in the Civic Centre, but separate, the Archives Service maintains the original Central Index of Merchant Seamen (1918–41) and there is an online guide explaining how to access and use this collection: www.southampton.gov.uk/s-leisure/artsheritage/history/maritimehistory/centralindex.aspx.

Guildhall Library and London Metropolitan Archives

www.cityoflondon.gov.uk/guildhalllibrary and www.cityoflondon.gov.uk/lma
The Guildhall holds the internationally important Lloyd's Marine Collection, including *Lloyd's List*, *Lloyd's Missing Vessel Books*

(1873–1954), and many other Lloyd's publications. There is a published guide to the collection: D.T. Barriskill, *Guide to the Lloyd's Marine Collection* (Guildhall Library, 2006). *Admiralty Wreck Registers* (1850-54) are also kept here, as well as Board of Trade *Wrecks and Casualties Returns* (1856–1918). The website has helpful research leaflets.

London Metropolitan Archives houses *Lloyd's Captains' Register*, and papers describing the awards of Lloyd's medals (from 1836). Their records for Trinity House in London include petitions for pensions by seafarers, and applications by merchant ship captains to pilot their own vessels.

Lloyd's Register Headquarters, London

www.lr.org

The headquarters holds a complete collection of *Lloyd's Register of Shipping* from 1764 to the present day, as well as *Lloyd's Register of Yachts* from 1878. There is also a good collection of books about individual shipping companies past and present, and this is the sole holder of 'Lloyd's Register Wreck Books' (1940–77).

Museums and Heritage Sites in the UK

Aberdeen Maritime Museum

www.aagm.co.uk

Concentrates on shipbuilding, fast sailing ships, fishing, and the history of Aberdeen as a port.

Cutty Sark, Greenwich, London

www.cuttysark.org.uk

Launched in 1869, *Cutty Sark* is the last remaining tea clipper in existence.

Docklands, Museum of London

www.museumindocklands.org.uk

Located inside a Georgian riverside warehouse, this museum tells the story of London as a port and includes a recreation of the Victorian backstreets near the docks.

Glenlee, Riverside Museum, Glasgow
www.thetallship.com
Launched in 1898, this is the only tall ship built on the Clyde that
is still afloat in the UK.

Historic Dockyard, Chatham
www.thedockyard.co.uk
Although a naval dockyard, this museum also tells the story of
shipbuilding and rope-making in the days of sail, and houses the
RNLI lifeboat collection.

HMS *Belfast*, Thames, London
http://hmsbelfast.iwm.org.uk
A Royal Navy ship that escorted Allied merchant ships in convoy
during the Second World War.

Maritime Experience, Hartlepool
www.hartlepoolsmaritimeexperience.com
Home of the 1930s steamship *Wingfield Castle*, and the famous
historic quayside which recreates the atmosphere of a port in days
gone by.

Merchant Navy Memorial, London
www.merchantnavymemorial.com
Commemorates over 36,000 merchant navy personnel who have
no grave but the sea, and who died serving their country in two
world wars.

Merseyside Maritime Museum, Liverpool
www.liverpoolmuseums.org.uk/maritime/
Focuses on the merchant navy and the history of Liverpool.
Galleries include the Battle of the Atlantic, the *Titanic* and the
Lusitania, and the story of emigration from Liverpool.

National Maritime Museum, Greenwich, London
www.nmm.ac.uk
The UK's premier museum devoted to the nation's maritime
heritage.

Sea City, Southampton
www.seacitymuseum.co.uk
Museum relaying the story of Southampton as one of the UK's most important maritime gateways. Includes an exploration of what life was like in the merchant service in the early twentieth century.

SS *Great Britain*, Bristol
www.ssgreatbritain.org
The largest ship afloat at her launch in 1843, Brunel's ship *Great Britain* was the first iron-hulled oceangoing passenger ship.

SS *Robin*, Thames, London
www.ssrobin.com
The world's oldest complete steamship, and the last surviving Victorian coastal cargo steamer.

National Historic Ships
There are ships of historical importance in the UK that are open to the public or privately owned. Visit the National Historic Ships database at www.nationalhistoricships.org.uk/ for a listing.

Places of Interest Outside the UK

There are opportunities to learn more about the history of the British merchant navy from heritage facilities in other countries. A selection of examples are given below.

Dunbrody, County Wexford, Eire
www.dunbrody.com
Explore conditions on board this replica of a Victorian sailing ship for Irish emigrants to the USA.

Edwin Fox, Picton, New Zealand
www.edwinfoxsociety.com
The last surviving vessel to have been used to carry convicts to Australia and as a Crimean War troopship. This British ship also carried merchant cargoes and immigrants to New Zealand.

James Craig, Sydney, Australia
www.shf.org.au/JCraig/JCraig.html
The only nineteenth-century British sailing ship that still makes
weekly voyages. You can book a day's voyage into the Pacific on
board this beautiful barque – an unbeatable experience if you have
Victorian merchant navy ancestors.

Maritime History Archive, Memorial University of Newfoundland, Canada
www.mun.ca/mha
Holds British ship crew lists from 1863 to 1976: the website allows
you to identify specific holdings pre-1938. Also holds registration,
voyage, and personnel records for Canadian ports that can relate to
British ships. You can visit, or pay for research to be conducted on
your behalf.

Maritime Museum of the Atlantic, Halifax, Canada
http://museum.gov.ns.ca/mmanew/en/home/default.aspx
Visit the exploration ship *Acadia*, which also served in two world
wars. Permanent exhibits include the stories of Nova Scotia's many
shipwrecks, and the importance of convoys in the Second World
War.

Plimoth Plantation, Massachusetts, USA
www.plimoth.org
Board a seaworthy replica of the seventeenth-century *Mayflower*, a
British cargo ship that was converted to carry the Pilgrim Fathers
as passengers, and explore the life of early emigrants to America.

Polly Woodside, Melbourne, Australia
www.pollywoodside.com.au
Launched at Belfast in 1885, this handsome sailing ship has been
restored to allow visitors on board.

Queen Mary, Long Beach, California, USA
www.queenmary.com
An opportunity to appreciate the elegance of the golden age of
transatlantic liners. You can use the ship as a hotel, dine on board,
or take a tour.

Star of India, San Diego, California, USA
www.sdmaritime.org
This British-built barque is the oldest active sailing ship in the world, being laid down in 1863. Voyages are now infrequent.

Western Australian Museum, Shipwreck Galleries, Fremantle, Australia
www.museum.wa.gov.au
The most extensive shipwreck museum in the southern hemisphere.

Chapter 9

CASE HISTORIES

Ipresent below five case histories which are common scenarios that family historians will encounter. There is always more than one way to approach the information-gathering exercise, but I have tried to present the process in a logical order. I hope that they could act as exemplars if you are faced with a similar situation, but they also illustrate how the various sources described in separate chapters of this book can be used together to form a complete picture of an ancestor's career or ship.

A Victorian Captain

William Leverett was born in Portsmouth in 1827, but lived partly in Devon. Family tales suggest he went to sea and eventually became captain of a vessel for a wealthy owner. He died in 1879. What is the best way to trace him?

A William Leverett of the right age was 'master mariner' in the 1861 and 1871 census for Portsmouth. He was on shore each time, so his ships are not recorded. No captain William Leverett could be found in *Lloyd's Register* for the 1850s and 1860s via GoogleBooks.

The Guildhall online index to *Lloyd's Captains' Register* shows William (born Portsmouth 1827) was awarded his master's certificate at Plymouth in 1858, so confirming a south-west England connection. His certificate number was C18039 F&A, showing that he could captain sailing ships only. The same number is given in the *Mercantile Navy List* for 1860.

His master's certificate and associated papers were ordered from the NMM. William wrote to complain that he did not need to sit an examination, because he had over fifteen years' experience at sea. This may also have been because he had been already calling himself a ship's master, as captain of the *Nymph*, without the necessary certificate. The Board of Trade wrote back, stiffly, that he had insufficient experience as a master and had to sit the exam. William reluctantly paid his two pounds fee and sat the sailing ships exam in Plymouth in 1858, and passed it.

William's application form reveals his whole seagoing career from the age of fourteen, when he was apprenticed on the *Argo*, until his examination. Between 1841 and 1857 he served on thirteen different ships based in Plymouth, Portsmouth, Cowes, and Dublin but his highest ranking was as mate. His full address and date of birth are given.

The entry for William in the Guildhall index to *Lloyd's Captains' Register* was followed up in the original registers at London Metropolitan Archives. This showed that he was master of the 42-ton yacht *Osprey* (ON 9891) from 1870 to 1875. The owner of the *Osprey* was indeed a wealthy man, as family stories suggested – the *Mercantile Navy List* for 1870 identifies him as Lord John Petre of Norfolk. The Maritime History Archive website showed that Portsmouth Records Office held the crew lists for the *Osprey* and, when consulted, these indicated that William became master of the vessel in January 1859 and continued until 1878. During this time he frequently took the Petre family on holiday to the Mediterranean, Scotland, and Ireland.

Finding a Victorian Ship

Hero was an 1830s merchant ship, possibly based at Poole, because its master, John Bell, lived there. How can I find out more about this ship? What did it look like and what happened to it?

It does not take long to look through all the 1830s editions of *Lloyd's Register* online, because the ships are listed alphabetically. The first mention of a Poole-based ship called *Hero* is in 1834, and it is subsequently listed every year until 1841. The master is recorded as 'J. Bell'. The *Hero* was a cargo-carrying brig of 165 tons that regularly sailed from Poole to America. It was a prize – a ship captured from the enemy during wartime – and was rated Æ1 by Lloyd's in 1834 after a major refit in 1833 (new deck, sheathing, and topsides).

The Guildhall's online index to *Lloyd's List* allows you to enter both ship's name and captain's surname as search terms. This reveals that John Bell had a tough time as captain of the *Hero*. The vessel was driven back to Bridport much damaged after a storm in late 1833, then had to be assisted into Harwich harbour in 1834 after suddenly springing a major leak. On 9 March 1835, she was driven off her anchorage by a storm and struck land near Lowestoffe, knocking out her rudder. Subsequent editions of the *List* recount that, although all the cargo and the crew was saved, the waves quickly smashed the *Hero* open and shattered the hull beyond repair. It was left to rot on the beach.

This illustrates one danger of relying on Victorian editions of *Lloyd's Register* as a sole source of information: they were not always updated speedily. In this case, the *Hero* continued to be listed as an active ship for six years after it was wrecked.

The *Hero's* registration document at TNA (BT 107/216) shows it was registered in Poole in May 1833, so the refit noted in *Lloyd's Register* was probably carried out at the shipyards there. The registration document notes that the *Hero* was a prize captured from the French in 1805 and was formerly called *Vigilante*. The ship had two masts, one deck, and no figurehead. It was 73 feet, 5½ inches long; at her broadest point she was 23 feet and 11 inches wide; the hold was thirteen feet and three inches deep. The owner, James Manlaws, died in 1833, and ownership passed to the executrix of his estate, Margaret Patzcker, so there may have been insufficient cash-flow to keep the ship in good repair given its age.

Last Days of Sail to First World War

Frederic Stanley Brown was born in Bury in 1871 and was a merchant navy captain in the Royal Fleet Auxiliary when he retired in 1931. What ships did he serve on in his career?

Frederic is not listed in the 1891 or 1911 census, but in 1901 he was cited as third mate on board SS *Minneapolis* at Tilbury Docks. He is not recorded as part of the fourth registration of merchant seamen (1918–41).

The index of certified officers, BT352, at TNA shows that he earned certificate number 026587, which was granted for the position of second mate in 1893, first mate in 1895, and master in 1899. Men often earned qualifications for higher ranks long before they could serve at that level – Frederic was still a third mate in the 1901 census.

His certificates and application forms for certificates were viewed at the NMM and they record his nineteenth-century career. He first went to sea in 1888 as a cadet on the *Stracathro*, which according to *Lloyd's Register* was a large sailing barque based in Dundee, but he made the change to steamships in the mid-1890s.

Frederic is also listed in *Lloyd's Captains' Register*, and this records his shipboard career from 1901, starting with SS *Minneapolis* identified from the census, and serving as mate on eight other ships until he was first mate on the *Trefoil* in 1920. According to this, he took up his first post as captain in 1921, on board the *Boxol*, then moved to the *War Krishna* in 1925, then *War Pathan* (1927).

There are some gaps in this record, particularly for 1916 to 1920, and for the period after 1928. Since his career for part of the First World War is missing, the *London Gazette* was searched online to determine if he received a commission in the RNR as an officer. Sure enough, 'Frederic S. Browne' is recorded as being appointed to the rank of temporary sub-lieutenant on 18 October 1916.

The RNR officers' index for Frederic Browne covering First World War service is ADM240/84 ('Abbott to Cartwright'). It shows that his RNR service records are given in volume 9, page 377. Using TNA's Catalogue, or the advanced search in the Discovery service, the original volume 9 now corresponds to RNR service records ADM 240/45. When ordered to view at TNA, page 377 reveals that Frederic's first appointment was on board the *Prestol*, and that his first post in charge was as RNR lieutenant in command of the *Boxol* in 1918 (three years before Lloyd's recorded his first captain's position). His behaviour is recorded as 'most zealous and capable', despite a prolonged spell of illness in 1918 which rendered him unfit for duty. His address is given as 6 Market Place, East Finchley.

The roll of RNR officers' medals (ADM171/92) shows Frederic was presented with the Victory Medal and the British War Medal. Furthermore, he is listed as a recipient of the Mercantile Marine Medal among the merchant navy medal recipients for the First World War at TNA (BT351/1). He did not receive an RNR Long Service Medal.

Frederic's service in the Royal Fleet Auxiliary was followed up on the Historical RFA website www.historicalrfa.org, and this provides photographs of some of his ships, including the *Boxol*. While on board this ship, he had to dismiss his own chief officer for being absent without leave. Additional commands not given in

Lloyd's Captains' Register include the *Servitor* and the *Scotol*. In 1927 he became master of the *Ebonol* until he retired in 1931.

Peacetime Shipping Disaster

An old family letter from 1908 recalls it being ten years since Henry Pinfold was lost in a shipping disaster that 'claimed the lives of so many'. Henry was a crewman, not a passenger, and born in 1869. What happened to him?

Without the name of the ship, such searches can be very difficult. However, assuming the year of 1898 for Henry's death is correct, then it is often best to determine first if a body was found. There is no record of a Henry Pinfold dying in the GRO index of marine deaths, nor in the index to overseas marine deaths, but the free index to GRO births, marriages, and deaths in the UK at www.freeBMD.org.uk lists a Henry Pinfold of the right age (twenty-nine years) dying in the last quarter of 1898. This means a body was retrieved.

The National Burials Index reveals a gravestone to a Henry Pinfold aged twenty-nine years at Mawnan Parish Church, Cornwall. The date of death is given as 14 October 1898. TNA's Registers and Indexes of Births, Marriages and Deaths of Passengers and Seamen at Sea dates from 1891 (BT334). The register for 1898 (BT334/18) identifies a Henry Pinfold dying at sea. He is recorded as a carpenter from Kent, who drowned aged twenty-eight, on board the *Mohegan* when it was wrecked off the coast near Falmouth on 14 October 1898. His address was 11 Peter Street, Gravesend.

Despite the *Mohegan* being a famous wreck, the crew lists for this ship have not been retained by TNA in its celebrated ships series (BT100). However, the CLIP website provides the *Mohegan's* official number of 109043. Using this, the surviving crew lists for the *Mohegan* from 1898 can be ordered from the Maritime History Archives in Newfoundland, and this confirms that Henry Pinfold was the ship's carpenter and identifies his crewmates.

Reports about the *Mohegan's* fate were published in many newspapers, for example in *The Times* of 17 October 1898. The *Graphic* has a particularly detailed account in its edition of 22 October 1898, featuring several photographs and sketches. A short book on the subject has also been written by Terry Moyle, *The Mohegan*

1898–1998 (Talbot Partnership, 1998). The vessel sank on only her third commercial voyage by steering a wrong course and crashing into rocks in calm weather. The ship went down in just fifteen minutes and the survivors were rescued by the lifeboat service; 106 passengers and crew were drowned.

The official inquiry into the disaster by the Board of Trade is kept at the Southampton Archives, but is available online at www .plimsoll.org. It lists all the crew and passengers who survived and those lost (including Henry), and incorporates great detail as well as interviews with many of Henry's colleagues. By typing 'Mohegan' into TNA's Catalogue/Discovery service and restricting to series MT, the Ministry of Transport's own papers about the disaster can also be retrieved by visiting TNA, and this provides some extra detail (MT9/602). In particular the ministry evidently did not think highly of the inquiry's recommendations to prevent future, similar tragedies.

The NMM Maritime Memorials database at www.nmm.ac.uk/ memorials does not identify a memorial to Henry but does note a large commemorative window to the disaster in St Keverne's Church which was installed by the shipowners. A headstone was also erected in the churchyard to mark the mass grave of the many people whose bodies were found, but who could not be identified.

Died in Second World War

Thomas Henry Warrington from Kent (born 1916) joined the merchant service. In the Second World War his family heard that he'd died at Christmas time. What more detail is available?

The Commonwealth War Graves Commission website identifies only one Thomas Henry Warrington who fought in the merchant service. He was a seaman, born in 1916 who died on 1 December 1940. He is commemorated on panel 9 of the Tower Hill memorial to the merchant navy. The panel itself discloses the ship he served on – the *Appalachee* – and that six other crewmen died with Thomas when the vessel was attacked. The GRO register of marine deaths via www.thegenealogist.co.uk also identifies a Thomas Henry Warrington of the *Appalachee* dying at sea, aged twenty-four.

The fourth register of merchant seamen, online via Find My Past, indicates that Thomas had previously served on coastal vessels before registering in 1935 while on the ship *Authority*. Thomas is described as being 5 feet and 6 inches tall, with blue eyes, light brown hair, and a medium complexion. He had his initials, 'THW', tattooed on his left forearm. He moved to the *British Mariner* in March 1940, before being transferred to the ill-fated *Appalachee* in July.

The *Appalachee* was an 8,826-ton tanker that was hit by a U-boat torpedo, according to the Battleship Cruisers website list of merchant navy casualties.

Convoy records at TNA (ADM199/2185) show that the *Appalachee* was part of a flotilla of forty-one ships crossing the Atlantic from Halifax to Liverpool as convoy HX 90. They departed on 21 November, but were attacked by a pack of U-boats beginning on the 1 December, the *Appalachee* being one of the first to be targeted. Eleven of the vessels were sunk.

Perusal of the Admiralty records of wartime merchant ship survivors reveals that the captain of the ship, William Armstrong, survived the attack and was interviewed by the Admiralty as soon as he reached shore. His account reveals the *Appalachee*'s fate in detail in ADM199/2135 at TNA. The ship was targeted by a U-boat as night fell and had its stern blown off, but thirty-two men survived.

The online Wrecksite database at www.wrecksite.eu specifies the current location of the wreck and provides a picture of the *Appalachee*. The U-boat website http://uboat.net also offers a photograph, describes the ship and its cargo (aviation fuel), as well as identifying the German submarine that sank her (U-101, commanded by Ernst Mengersen).

BIBLIOGRAPHY

Barriskill, D.T., *Guide to the Lloyd's Marine Collection*, Guildhall Library, 2006.

Bowen, F.C., *History of the Royal Naval Reserve*, Corporation of Lloyds, 1926.

Cook, G.C., *Disease in the Merchant Navy: A History of the Seamen's Hospital Society*, Radcliffe Publishing Ltd, 2007.

Cox, B., *Lifeboat Gallantry: The Complete Record of Royal National Lifeboat Institution Gallantry Medals and How They Were Won 1824–1996*, Spink & Son, 1998.

Earle, P., *Sailors: English Merchant Seamen 1650–1775*, Methuen, 1998.

Gawler, J., *Lloyd's Medals 1836–1989*, Howell Press, 1995.

Graves, J., *Waterline: Images from the Golden Age of Cruising*, National Maritime Museum, 2005.

Greenway, A., *The Cargo Liners: An Illustrated History*, Seaforth Publishing, 2009.

Hocking, C., *Dictionary of Disasters at Sea During the Age of Steam 1824–1962*, Naval & Military Press, reprint 1994.

Huntress, K.G., *A Checklist of Narratives of Shipwrecks and Disasters at Sea 1586 to 1860*, Iowa State University Press, 1979.

Johnson, D.S. and J. Nurminen, *The History of Seafaring: Navigating the World's Oceans*, Conway Maritime Press, 2007.

Larn, R. and B., *Shipwreck Index of the British Isles*, Lloyd's Register, 1995–2002, 6 vols.

MacGregor, D., *Merchant Sailing Ships*, Conway Maritime Press,

1984–5, 3 vols (Vol. 1: 1775–1815; Vol. 2: 1815–50; Vol. 3: 1850–75).

Pappalardo, B. *Tracing Your Naval Ancestors*, Public Record Office, 2003.

Talbot-Booth, E.C., *His Majesty's Merchant Navy*, Sampson Low, Marston & Co., various editions dating from 1941.

Talbot-Booth, E.C., *Ships and the Sea*, Sampson Low, Marston & Co., various editions dating from 1936.

Villiers, A., *Square-Rigged Ships: An Introduction*, National Maritime Museum, 2009.

Watson, M.H., *Disasters at Sea: Every Ocean-Going Passenger Ship Catastrophe Since 1900*, Patrick Stephens, 1995.

Williams, A., *The Battle of the Atlantic*, BBC Worldwide, 2002.

Woodman, R., *A History of the British Merchant Navy*, The History Press, 5 vols (Vol. 1: *Neptune's Trident, 1500–1807* (2008); Vol. 2: *Britannia's Realm, 1763–1815* (2009); Vol. 3: *Masters Under God, 1816–1884* (2009); Vol. 4: *More Days, More Dollars, 1885–1920* (2010); Vol. 5: *Fiddler's Green, 1921–2010* (2010)).

Woodman, R., *The History of the Ship*, Conway Maritime Press, 1997.

ABBREVIATIONS

DisA number	discharge number
GRO	General Register Office
GRT	gross register tonnage
MHA	Maritime History Archive
MNL	*Mercantile Navy List*
NMM	National Maritime Museum
NUS	National Union of Seamen
PCC	Prerogative Court of Canterbury
RFA	Royal Fleet Auxiliary
RGSS	Registrar General of Shipping and Seamen
RHS	Royal Humane Society
RN	Royal Navy
RND	Royal Naval Division
RNLI	Royal National Lifeboat Institute
RNR	Royal Naval Reserve
RNVR	Royal Naval Volunteer Reserve
TNA	The National Archives

INDEX

Page numbers in italics refer to illustrations

Tracing your family tree?

Read Your Family HISTORY

OUR EXPERTS YOUR STORIES

Your Family History is the family history magazine from Dr Nick Barratt and his research team. It is essential reading for all family, local and military historians. The aim of the magazine is to get real people involved and we have the best experts and the best advice for all your family history needs. We want to feature YOUR stories, YOUR discoveries, YOUR mysteries and YOUR documents. Each issue features a beginner's guide, up-to-date news on all the latest online releases, ask the experts, a reader's story, a spotlight on a local area and regular features such as news, events, reviews of books and software and more.

Out now at all good newsagents or SUBSCRIBE TODAY AND RECEIVE:

- A **FREE** copy of Nick Barratt's *Guide to Your Ancestors Lives* worth **£19.99**

- **Save up to 25%** off the cover price when you subscribe by Direct Debit

- Offers and discounts in our Subscriber Zone

- Join the *Your Family History* Forum

www.your-familyhistory.com